Lawrence A. Cremin, General Editor

☆ ☆ ☆

Number 1

THE REPUBLIC AND THE SCHOOL

Horace Mann on the Education of Free Men

Edited by Lawrence A. Cremin

Number 2

AMERICAN IDEAS ABOUT ADULT EDUCATION

1710-1951

Edited by C. Hartley Grattan

Number 3

DEWEY ON EDUCATION

Selections with an Introduction and Notes

by Martin S. Dworkin

Number 4

THE SUPREME COURT AND EDUCATION

Edited by David Fellman

Number 5

INTERNATIONAL EDUCATION

A Documentary History

Edited by David G. Scanlon

Number 6

CRUSADE AGAINST IGNORANCE

Thomas Jefferson on Education

Edited by Gordon C. Lee

SERIES PREFACE

"It is, of course, quite true that the responsibility for public education is primarily the concern of the States, but it is equally true that such responsibilities, like all other state activity, must be exercised consistently with federal constitutional requirements as they apply to state action." Thus has the United States Supreme Court defined one of the central political problems of our time: the task of reconciling the traditional localism of American education with the rights and liberties guaranteed by the Fourteenth Amendment to the Federal Constitution. In a score of recent opinions, most of them handed down since 1945, the Court has worked resolutely at this task, with prodigious results for schools at all levels. Professor Fellman has gathered together excerpts from the more important of these opinions—minority as well as majority—with a view to illuminating both the constitutional and the educational issues at stake. Readers will find here much more than formal legalistic argument; for the Court's opinions have embodied some of the most cogent and compelling discussions of educational policy set before the American public in recent years.

Lawrence A. Cremin

The SUPREME COURT and EDUCATION

Edited, with an introduction and notes, by

DAVID FELLMAN

BUREAU OF PUBLICATIONS
TEACHERS COLLEGE, COLUMBIA UNIVERSITY
NEW YORK

Library of Congress Catalog Card
Number 60-8488

Second printing, 1961

Printed in the United States of America

Contents

Introduction

In the American federal system, education has always been primarily a function of the states and their local subdivisions. The national government, under the United States Constitution, is limited to the delegated powers enumerated therein, and no authority over education is given to it. Congress does have the power to "lay and collect taxes" in order "to pay the debts and provide for the common defence and general welfare of the United States," and the promotion of education is clearly for the country's general welfare. Accordingly, various forms of federal aid to education take the form of expenditures authorized by Congress to promote the general welfare. In addition, Congress may give financial aid for education to carry out any other delegated power. Thus the most recent great statute, which extends a variety of forms of financial assistance for education—the National Defense Education Act of 1958—was adopted to implement, from the legal point of view, the extensive national defense powers vested in Congress by the Constitution.

The oldest federal grant for educational purposes was the Land Ordinance of 1785, which set aside the sixteenth section of every township in the western territory "for the maintenance of public schools within the said township." Probably the most influential federal grant for educational purposes to date was the Morrill Act of 1862 which created the land-grant colleges. Congress gave to the states many millions of acres of public land for the support of colleges offering programs in agriculture, engineering, and home economics. Since 1890 Congress has made regular annual appropriations of money for the promotion of education in the agricultural colleges. This educational program has been supplemented, since 1914, when the Smith-Lever Act was adopted, with federal support for the Agricultural Extension Service.

While Congress may spend money for the promotion of education, and attach conditions to its expenditures, it has no direct power to fix the standards of education except in those areas where it has direct legislative power —the District of Columbia, the territories and other possessions, and federal enclaves, such as forts and other military installations. The Office of Education, established by Congress in 1867, and since 1953 located in the Department of Health, Education, and Welfare, collects educational statistics, conducts research, advises and consults with state and local school officials, and administers various grants-in-aid to education and special programs. The Office also administers the national vocational education acts and the National Defense Education Act of 1958.

Actually, the commitments of the national government in the field of education are now considerable. On the international level it participates in the United Nations Educational, Scientific and Cultural Organization (UNESCO), maintains an international educational exchange service, gives technical assistance to foreign countries in various areas of educational activity, administers student visa problems, and supervises the admission to American institutions of foreign students. On the national level the federal government has a wide variety of educational programs dealing with agriculture, the teaching of citizenship, education for the blind and the deaf, civil defense, health and nutrition, Indians, fisheries, botanical studies, various basic sciences, veterans, vocational training, and wildlife conservation. In addition it maintains a number of service academies for the military establishments.

But however considerable federal activity may be, it is still true that the national government has relatively little to do with most of the country's educational system. The overwhelming majority of American students attend schools maintained by local school boards which function under the authority of state law. A considerable minority of students attend private schools which have only minimal connections with any government. The impact of the national government through legislation and appropriation upon the American educational system is at most tangential and indirect. The states and their local subdivisions, mainly school districts, support most of our schools through local taxation, and fix their own standards of operation. These are not, for the most part, matters of federal concern at all.

The United States Constitution, however, is the supreme law of the land, and as such is ultimately enforceable by the Supreme Court. Insofar as the Constitution imposes limitations on the states, the states are bound by them, and by the interpretations which the Supreme Court attaches to them.

Before the Civil War there was nothing in the federal Constitution which set limits to what the states could do in the field of education. If any one had a grievance so far as a local educational activity was concerned, he had to be content with whatever appeals he could take within his state's judicial system. While the federal Bill of Rights has a number of provisions which might have a bearing on educational policy—such as the guaranty of religious freedom in the First Amendment, and of due process of law in the Fifth—it was established by the Supreme Court at a very early date, in *Barron* v. *Baltimore,* 7 Pet. 243 (1833), that the Bill of Rights was not intended to apply as limitations upon the states, but only upon the national government. If, for example, a state did something before the Civil War violative of one's religious freedom, he had no appeal beyond his highest state court. For state courts speak with finality regarding the meaning of state law, and the national Supreme Court may review state courts only where federal questions of law are involved.

A very drastic change was made in this traditional division of national and state power in 1868, when the states ratified the Fourteenth Amendment as one of the major legal consequences of the Civil War. This Amendment imposed on the states very broadly phrased limitations for the purpose of protecting the rights of individuals. "No State," Section 1 of the Fourteenth

Amendment decrees, "shall make or enforce any law which shall abridge the privileges or immunities of citizens of the United States; nor shall any State deprive any person of life, liberty, or property, without due process of law; nor deny to any person within its jurisdiction the equal protection of the laws." What these sweeping clauses mean is a matter of interpretation, and ultimately for the Supreme Court to decide authoritatively and with finality.

The first of the three clauses of Section 1—which forbids the abridgment by the states of the privileges or immunities of United States citizens—got off to a bad start in the *Slaughterhouse Cases,* 16 Wall. 36 (1873), and has never amounted to very much, since the Court insisted on drawing a basic distinction between federal and state privileges and immunities, holding that the latter did not fall within the scope of the limitation. But the due process and equal protection clauses, which got off to a slow start, have become through a gradual process of interpretation the most important of all constitutional provisions from the point of view of federally enforceable limitations on the states.

It was not until 1925 that the Supreme Court ruled squarely, in *Gitlow* v. *New York,* 268 U.S. 652, that one of the liberties which states may not invade unreasonably and arbitrarily, in violation of the Due Process Clause, is the liberty of speech. In 1940, in *Cantwell* v. *Connecticut,* 310 U.S. 296, the Court held, for the first time, that freedom of religion is one of the liberties which falls within the ambit of the due process guaranty. In fact, today all the great guaranties of the First Amendment—freedom of religion, separation of church and state, freedom of speech and of the press, and the right of association—are treated by the Court as falling within the scope of the Due Process Clause of the Fourteenth Amendment. The Court has consistently refused to hold that the Fourteenth Amendment was intended to nationalize all the guaranties of the federal Bill of Rights as limitations upon the states (*Adamson* v. *California,* 332 U.S. 46 [1947]), and thus some of the purely procedural clauses, such as those dealing with the jury system, do not apply to the states. But those clauses which have implications for education do apply to the states. If, for example, a state adopts a regulation for school children which violates their religious freedom, a federal remedy is available through appeal to the Supreme Court.

Although the limitations of the Fourteenth Amendment apply only to state action—"no State shall"—it is important to note that the Supreme Court takes a broad view of what constitutes state action. There is state action, of course, if the legislature passes a law, but there is also state action if the act is that of the governor or some other executive officer, or of a state board or commission, or of a state court, or of any county, city, village, school board or other local governmental body. In fact, any policeman who holds office by virtue of state law, or purports to act pursuant to state law, falls within the scope of the concept of state action. Whoever acts under color of state law is acting for the state and is therefore subject to the restraints of the Fourteenth Amendment.

So far as the field of education is concerned, the cases which the United States Supreme Court has decided fall into three groups. One group deals with the impact of state educational policy on claims to religious liberty. A second series has dealt with the ever-thorny question of racial segregation in the public schools. The third group of cases, a very small group, has been concerned with issues of academic freedom.

Educational policy often impinges on claims of religious conscience. In the first great Supreme Court decision on this subject, *Pierce* v. *Society of Sisters* (p. 1), the Court had to face the question whether there was a federal constitutional right to operate a religious-oriented parochial school in the face of a state policy which was designed to compel all children to attend public schools through the eighth grade. Whether a taxpayer's property is taken without due process of law by supplying textbooks (*Cochran* v. *Louisiana State Board of Education,* p. 5), or bus rides (*Everson* v. *Board of Education,* p. 9), at public expense to students attending private schools has been adjudicated by the nation's highest court. It has also ruled on the right of a local school board to compel school children to salute the flag and recite a pledge where such a ceremony is contrary to religious belief (*West Virginia State Board of Education* v. *Barnette,* p. 31). Perhaps the most widely debated subject today is that of the use of public school facilities or school time for religious education. Here a position taken by the Court, in *Illinois ex rel. McCollum* v. *Board of Education* (p. 45), aroused such a tremendous amount of controversy that the Court quickly withdrew to a less vulnerable position, in *Zorach* v. *Clauson* (p. 57).

Whether racial segregation in the public schools is constitutional depends on how the Equal Protection Clause of the Fourteenth Amendment is interpreted. It is impossible to determine what the authors and ratifiers of the Fourteenth Amendment had in mind on this subject, since the public school system we now have scarcely existed at that time. The Supreme Court committed itself, in 1896, in the well known case of *Plessy* v. *Ferguson,* 163 U.S. 537, to the proposition that the maintenance of racially separated transportation facilities did not violate the Equal Protection Clause so long as the facilities were equal. This marked the beginning of the stormy career of the "separate but equal" doctrine, but it is worth emphasizing that the *Plessy* decision was concerned with transportation and not with education.

Those who wished to break down the racial barriers which many state legislatures erected in the public schools had their first victories in the field of higher education. Thus in 1938 the Supreme Court held that Missouri could not legally close the state university's law school to Negroes by paying the tuition of resident Negroes to attend the law schools of other states (*Missouri ex rel. Gaines* v. *Canada,* 305 U.S. 337). Speaking for the Court, Chief Justice Hughes asserted that "manifestly, the obligations of the state to give the protection of equal laws can be performed only where its laws operate, that is, within its own jurisdiction. It is there that the equality of legal rights must be maintained." Ten years later the Supreme Court ordered open for a Negro student the doors of the School of Law of the University of Oklahoma (*Sipuel* v. *Board of Education,* 332 U.S. 631 [1948]), and in 1950 the Court rejected an attempt of the state of Texas actually to create a separate law school for Negro students, in *Sweatt* v. *Painter* (p. 69). The great climax came when principles already established for higher education were applied to the grade schools in the spring of 1954 (*Brown* v. *Board of Education,* p. 75). The riotous events in Little Rock only served to stiffen the attitude of the Justices (*Cooper* v. *Aaron,* p. 85).

Questions of academic freedom are rarely litigated in our courts. For the most part, academic freedom does not even fall within the scope of the legal protection which is available to parties who go to court. It depends on administrative practices and understandings, and falls outside the formal system of legal rights. Where issues involving academic freedom can be litigated at all, the outcome normally depends on the interpretation of state law by state courts. But in very recent years, as a consequence of a rather excited search for security in a dangerous world, a few appeals have reached the Supreme Court in which the issue was basically one of academic freedom. A teacher whose job has been taken from him arbitrarily or whose freedom to teach has been invaded unreasonably does have a due process issue which he can seek to take to the United States Supreme Court. Although a few parties have succeeded in getting their appeals considered, the Court has been most reluctant to limit the state's power to fix the qualifications of teachers (*Adler* v. *Board of Education of New York,* p. 97), and to inquire into their fitness to teach (*Beilan* v. *Board of Education of Philadelphia,* p. 105). Furthermore the power of Congressional committees to carry on investigations in the field of education was affirmed in 1959 in very sweeping terms, in *Barenblatt* v. *United States* (p. 113).

DAVID FELLMAN

Madison, Wisconsin
July 1959

Part I

EDUCATION AND RELIGION

1

Pierce v. Society of Sisters

268 U.S. 510 (1925)

Appeals from the District Court of the U.S. for the District of Oregon.

MR. JUSTICE MCREYNOLDS delivered the opinion of a unanimous Court.

These appeals are from decrees, based upon undenied allegations, which granted preliminary orders restraining appellants from threatening or attempting to enforce the Compulsory Education Act adopted November 7, 1922, under the initiative provision of her Constitution by the voters of Oregon.

The challenged Act, effective September 1, 1926, requires every parent, guardian or other person having control or charge or custody of a child between eight and sixteen years to send him to "a public school for the period of time a public school shall be held during the current year" in the district where the child resides; and failure so to do is declared a misdemeanor. There are exemptions—not specially important here—for children who are not normal, or who have completed the eighth grade, or who reside at considerable distances from any public school, or whose parents or guardians hold special permits from the County Superintendent. The manifest purpose is to compel general attendance at public schools by normal children, between eight and sixteen, who have not completed the eighth grade. And without doubt enforcement of the statute would seriously impair, perhaps destroy, the profitable features of appellees' business and greatly diminish the value of their property.

Appellee, the Society of Sisters, is an Oregon corporation, organized in 1880, with power to care for orphans, educate and instruct the youth, establish and maintain academies or schools, and acquire necessary real and personal property. It has long devoted its property and effort to the secular and religious education and care of children, and has acquired the valuable good will of many parents and guardians. It conducts interdependent primary and high schools and junior colleges, and maintains orphanages for the custody and control of children between eight and sixteen. In its primary schools many children between those ages are taught the subjects usually pursued in Oregon public schools during the first eight years. Systematic religious instruction and moral training according to the tenets of the Roman Catholic Church are also regularly provided. . . .

No question is raised concerning the power of the State reasonably to regulate all schools, to inspect, supervise and examine them, their teachers and pupils; to require that all children of proper age attend some school, that teachers shall be of good moral character and patriotic disposition, that certain studies plainly essential to good citizenship must be taught, and that nothing be taught which is manifestly inimical to the public welfare.

The inevitable practical result of enforcing the Act under consideration would be destruction of appellees' primary schools, and perhaps all other private primary schools for normal children within the State of Oregon. These parties are engaged in a kind of undertaking not inherently harmful, but long regarded as useful and meritorious. Certainly there is nothing in the present records to indicate that they have failed to discharge their obligations to patrons, students or the State. And there are no peculiar circumstances or present emergencies which demand extraordinary measures relative to primary education.

Under the doctrine of *Meyer* v. *Nebraska,* 262 U.S. 390, we think it entirely plain that the Act of 1922 unreasonably interferes with the liberty of parents and guardians to direct the upbringing and education of children under their control. As often heretofore pointed out, rights guaranteed by the Constitution may not be abridged by legislation which has no reasonable relation to some purpose within the competency of the State. The fundamental theory of liberty upon which all governments in this Union repose excludes any general power of the State to standardize its children by forcing them to accept instruction from public teachers only. The child is not the mere creature of the State; those who nurture him and direct his destiny have the right, coupled with the high duty, to recognize and prepare him for additional obligations.

The decrees below are *affirmed*.

2

Cochran v. Louisiana State Board of Education

281 U.S. 370 (1930)

Appeal from the Supreme Court of Louisiana.

MR. CHIEF JUSTICE HUGHES delivered the opinion of a unanimous Court.

The appellants, as citizens and taxpayers of the State of Louisiana, brought this suit to restrain the State Board of Education and other state officials from expending any part of the severance tax fund in purchasing school books and in supplying them free of cost to the school children of the State, under Acts No. 100 and No. 143 of 1928, upon the ground that the legislation violated specified provisions of the constitution of the State, and also section 4 of Article IV and the Fourteenth Amendment of the Federal Constitution. The Supreme Court of the State affirmed the judgment of the trial court, which refused to issue an injunction.

Act No. 100 of 1928 provided that the severance tax fund of the State, after allowing funds and appropriations as required by the state constitution, should be devoted, "first, to supplying school books to the school children of the State." The Board of Education was directed to provide "school books for school children free of cost to such children." Act No. 143 of 1928 made appropriations in accordance with the above provisions.

The Supreme Court of the State, . . . held that these acts were not repugnant to either the state or the Federal Constitution.

No substantial Federal question is presented under section 4 of Article IV of the Federal Constitution guaranteeing to every State a republican form of government, as questions arising under this provision are political, not judicial, in character. . . .

The contention of the appellant under the Fourteenth Amendment is that taxation for the purchase of school books constituted a taking of private property for a private purpose. . . . The purpose is said to be to aid private, religious, sectarian and other schools not embraced in the public educational system of the State by furnishing textbooks free to the children attending such private schools. The operation and effect of the legislation in question were described by the Supreme Court of the State as follows:

> One may scan the acts in vain to ascertain where any money is appropriated for the purchase of school books for the use of any church, private, sectarian or even public school. The appropriations were made for the specific purpose of purchasing school books for the use of the school children of the state, free of cost to them. It was for their benefit and the resulting benefit to the state that the appropriations were made. True, these children attend some school, public or private, the latter, sectarian or nonsectarian, and that the books are to be furnished them for their use, free of cost, whichever they attend. The schools, however, are not the beneficiaries of these appropriations. They obtain nothing from them, nor are they relieved of a single obligation because of them. The school children and the state alone are the beneficiaries. It is also true that the sectarian schools, which some of the children attend, instruct their pupils in religion, and books are used for that purpose, but one may search diligently the acts, though without result, in an effort to find anything to the effect that it is the purpose of the state to furnish religious books for the use of such children. . . . What the statutes contemplate is that the same books that are furnished children attending public schools shall be furnished children attending private schools. This is the only practical way of interpreting and executing the statutes, and this is what the state board of education is doing. Among these books, naturally, none is to be expected, adapted to religious instruction.

The Court also stated, although the point is not of importance in relation to the Federal question, that it was "only the use of the books that is granted to the children, or, in other words, the books are lent to them."

Viewing the statute as having the effect thus attributed to it, we cannot doubt that the taxing power of the state is exerted for a public purpose. The legislation does not segregate private schools, or their pupils, as its beneficiaries or attempt to interfere with any matters of exclusively private concern. Its interest is education, broadly; its method, comprehensive. Individual interests are aided only as the common interest is safeguarded.

Judgment affirmed.

3

Everson v. Board of Education

330 U.S. 1 (1947)

Appeal from the Court of Errors and Appeals of New Jersey

MR. JUSTICE BLACK delivered the opinion of the Court.

A New Jersey statute authorizes its local school districts to make rules and contracts for the transportation of children to and from schools. The appellee, a township board of education, acting pursuant to this statute, authorized reimbursement to parents of money expended by them for the bus transportation of their children on regular buses operated by the public transportation system. Part of this money was for the payment of transportation of some children in the community to Catholic parochial schools. These church schools give their students, in addition to secular education, regular religious instruction conforming to the religious tenets and modes of worship of the Catholic Faith. The superintendent of these schools is a Catholic priest.

The appellant, in his capacity as a district taxpayer, filed suit in a state court challenging the right of the Board to reimburse parents of parochial school students. He contended that the statute and the resolution passed pursuant to it violated both the State and the Federal Constitutions. That court held that the legislature was without power to authorize such payment under the state constitution. . . . The New Jersey Court of Errors and Appeals reversed, holding that neither the statute nor the resolution passed pursuant to it was in conflict with the State constitution or the provisions of the Federal Constitution in issue.

Since there has been no attack on the statute on the ground that a part of its language excludes children attending private schools operated for profit from enjoying State payment for their transportation, we need not consider this exclusionary language; it has no relevancy to any constitutional question here presented. Furthermore, if the exclusion clause had been properly challenged, we do not know whether New Jersey's highest court would construe its statutes as precluding payment of the school transportation of any group of pupils, even those of a private school run for profit. Consequently, we put to one side the question as to the validity of the statute against the claim that it does not authorize payment for the transportation generally of school children in New Jersey.

The only contention here is that the state statute and the resolution, insofar as they authorized reimbursement to parents of children attending parochial schools, violate the Federal Constitution in these two respects, which to some extent overlap. *First.* They authorize the State to take by taxation the private property of some and bestow it upon others, to be used for their own private purposes. This, it is alleged, violates the due process clause of the Fourteenth Amendment. *Second.* The statute and the resolution forced inhabitants to pay taxes to help support and maintain schools which are dedicated to, and which regularly teach, the Catholic Faith. This is alleged to be a use of state power to support church schools contrary to the prohibition of the First Amendment which the Fourteenth Amendment made applicable to the states.

First. The due process argument that the state law taxes some people to help others carry out their private purposes is framed in two phases. The first phase is that a state cannot tax A to reimburse B for the cost of transporting his children to church schools. This is said to violate the due process clause because the children are sent to these church schools to satisfy the personal desires of their parents, rather than the public's interest in the general education of all children. This argument, if valid, would apply equally to prohibit state payment for the transportation of children to any nonpublic school, whether operated by a church or any other nongovernment individual or group. But, the New Jersey legislature has decided that a public purpose will be served by using tax-raised funds to pay the bus fares of all school children, including those who attend parochial schools. The New Jersey Court of Errors and Appeals has reached the same conclusion. The fact that a state law, passed to satisfy a public need, coincides with the personal desires of the individuals most directly affected is certainly an inadequate reason for us to say that a legislature has erroneously appraised the public need.

It is true that this Court has, in rare instances, struck down state statutes on the ground that the purpose for which tax-raised funds were to be expended was not a public one. . . . But the Court has also pointed out that this far-reaching authority must be exercised with the most extreme caution. *Green* v. *Frazier,* 253 U.S. 233, 240. Otherwise, a state's power to legislate for the public welfare might be seriously curtailed, a power which is a primary reason for the existence of states. Changing local conditions create new local problems which may lead a state's people and its local authorities to believe that laws authorizing new types of public services are necessary to promote the general well-being of the people. The Fourteenth Amendment did not strip the states of their power to meet problems previously left for individual solution. . . .

It is much too late to argue that legislation intended to facilitate the opportunity of children to get a secular education serves no public purpose. . . . The same thing is no less true of legislation to reimburse needy parents, or all parents, for payment of the fares of their children so that they can ride in public buses to and from schools rather than run the risk of traffic and other hazards incident to walking or "hitchhiking." . . . Nor does it follow that a law has a private rather than a public purpose because it provides that tax-raised funds will be paid to reimburse individuals on account of money spent by them in a way which furthers a public program. . . . Subsidies and loans to individuals such as farmers and home-owners, and to privately owned transportation systems, as well as many other kinds of businesses, have been commonplace practices in our state and national history.

Insofar as the second phase of the due process argument may differ from the first, it is by suggesting that taxation for transportation of children to church schools constitutes support of a religion by the State. But if the law is invalid for this reason, it is because it violates the First Amendment's prohibition against the establishment of religion by law. This is the exact question raised by appellant's second contention, to consideration of which we now turn.

Second. The New Jersey statute is challenged as a "law respecting an establishment of religion." The First Amendment, as made applicable to the states by the Fourteenth, *Murdock* v. *Pennsylvania,* 319 U.S. 105, commands that a state "shall make no law respecting an establishment of religion, or prohibiting the free exercise thereof." These words of the First Amendment reflected in the minds of early Americans a vivid mental picture of conditions and practices which they fervently wished to stamp out in order to preserve liberty for themselves and for their posterity. Doubtless their goal has not been entirely reached; but so far has the Nation moved toward it that the expression "law respecting an establishment of religion," probably does not so vividly remind present-day Americans of the evils, fears, and political problems that caused that expression to be written into our Bill of Rights. Whether this New Jersey law is one respecting an "establishment of religion" requires an understanding of the meaning of that language, particularly with respect to the imposition of taxes. Once again, therefore, it is not inappropriate briefly to review the background and environment of the period in which that constitutional language was fashioned and adopted.

A large proportion of the early settlers of this country came here from Europe to escape the bondage of laws which compelled them to support and attend government-favored churches. The centuries immediately before and contemporaneous with the colonization of

America had been filled with turmoil, civil strife, and persecutions, generated in large part by established sects determined to maintain their absolute political and religious supremacy. With the power of government supporting them, at various times and places, Catholics had persecuted Protestants, Protestants had persecuted Catholics, Protestant sects had persecuted other Protestant sects, Catholics of one shade of belief had persecuted Catholics of another shade of belief, and all of these had from time to time persecuted Jews. In efforts to force loyalty to whatever religious group happened to be on top and in league with the government of a particular time and place, men and women had been fined, cast in jail, cruelly tortured, and killed. Among the offenses for which these punishments had been inflicted were such things as speaking disrespectfully of the views of ministers of government-established churches, nonattendance at those churches, expressions of nonbelief in their doctrines, and failure to pay taxes and tithes to support them.

These practices of the old world were transplanted to and began to thrive in the soil of the new America. The very charters granted by the English Crown to the individuals and companies designated to make the laws which would control the destinies of the colonials authorized these individuals and companies to erect religious establishments which all, whether believers or nonbelievers, would be required to support and attend. An exercise of this authority was accompanied by a repetition of many of the old-world practices and persecutions. Catholics found themselves hounded and proscribed because of their faith; Quakers who followed their conscience went to jail; Baptists were peculiarly obnoxious to certain dominant Protestant sects; men and women of varied faiths who happened to be in a minority in a particular locality were persecuted because they steadfastly persisted in worshiping God only as their own consciences dictated. And all of these dissenters were compelled to pay tithes and taxes to support government-sponsored churches whose ministers preached inflammatory sermons designed to strengthen and consolidate the established faith by generating a burning hatred against dissenters.

These practices became so commonplace as to shock the freedom-loving colonials into a feeling of abhorrence. The imposition of taxes to pay ministers' salaries and to build and maintain churches and church property aroused their indignation. It was these feelings which found expression in the First Amendment. No one locality and no one group throughout the Colonies can rightly be given entire credit for having aroused the sentiment that culminated in adoption of the Bill of Rights' provisions embracing religious liberty. But Virginia, where the established church had achieved a dominant influence in political affairs and where many excesses attracted wide public attention, provided a great stimulus and able leadership for the movement. The people there, as elsewhere, reached the conviction that individual religious liberty could be achieved best under a government which was stripped of all power to tax, to support, or otherwise to assist any or all religions, or to interfere with the beliefs of any religious individual or group.

The movement toward this end reached its dramatic climax in Virginia in 1785-86 when the Virginia legislative body was about to renew Virginia's tax levy for the support of the established church. Thomas Jefferson and James Madison led the fight against this tax. Madison wrote his great Memorial and Remonstrance against the law. In it, he eloquently argued that a true religion did not need the support of law; that no person, either believer or nonbeliever, should be taxed to support a religious institution of any kind; that the best interest of a society required that the minds of men always be wholly free; and that cruel persecutions were the inevitable result of government-established religions. Madison's Remonstrance received strong support throughout Virginia, and the Assembly postponed consideration of the proposed tax measure until its next session. When the proposal came up for consideration at that session, it not only died in committee, but the Assembly enacted the famous "Virginia Bill for Religious Liberty" originally written by Thomas Jefferson. . . .

The "establishment of religion" clause of the First Amendment means at least this: Neither a state nor the Federal Government can set up a church. Neither can pass laws which aid one religion, aid all religions, or prefer one religion over another. Neither can force nor influence a person to go to or to remain away from church against his will or force him to profess a belief or disbelief in any religion. No person can be punished for entertaining or professing religious beliefs or disbeliefs, for church attendance or nonattendance. No tax in any amount, large or small, can be levied to support any religious activities or institutions, whatever they may be called, or whatever form they may adopt to teach or practice religion. Neither a state nor the Federal Government can, openly or secretly, participate in the affairs of any religious organizations or groups and *vice versa.* In the words of Jefferson, the clause against establishment of religion by law was intended to erect "a wall of separation between church and State."

We must consider the New Jersey statute in accordance with the foregoing limitations imposed by the First Amendment. But we must not strike that state statute down if it is within the State's constitutional power even though it approaches the verge of that power. . . . New Jersey cannot consistently with the "establishment of religion" clause of the First Amendment contribute tax-raised funds to the support of an institution which teaches the tenets and faith of any church. On the other hand, other language of the amendment commands that New Jersey cannot hamper its citizens in the free exercise of their own religion. Consequently, it cannot exclude individual Catholics, Lutherans, Mohammedans, Baptists, Jews, Methodists, Non-believers, Presbyterians, or the members of any other faith, *because of their faith, or lack of it,* from receiving the benefits of public welfare legislation. While we do not mean to intimate that a state could not provide transportation only to children attending public schools, we must be careful, in protecting the citizens of New Jersey against state-established churches, to be sure that we do not inadvertently prohibit New Jersey from extending its general state law benefits to all its citizens without regard to their religious belief.

Measured by these standards, we cannot say that the First Amendment prohibits New Jersey from spending tax-raised funds to pay the bus fares of parochial school pupils as a part of a general program under which it pays the fares of pupils attending public and other schools. It is undoubtedly true that children are helped to get to church schools. There is even a possibility that some of the children might not be sent to the church schools if the parents were compelled to pay their children's bus fares out of their own pockets when transportation to a public school would have been paid for by the State. The same possibility exists where the state requires a local transit company to provide reduced fares to school children including those attending parochial schools, or where a municipally owned transportation system undertakes to carry all school children free of charge. Moreover, state-paid policemen, detailed to protect children going to and from church schools from the very real hazards of traffic, would serve much the same purpose and accomplish much the same result as state provisions intended to guarantee free transportation of a kind which the state deems to be best for the school children's welfare. And parents might refuse to risk their children to the serious danger of traffic accidents going to and from parochial schools, the approaches to which were not protected by policemen. Similarly, parents might be reluctant to permit their children to attend schools which the state had cut off from such general government services as ordinary police and fire protection, connections for sewage disposal, public highways and sidewalks. Of course, cutting off church schools from these services, so separate and so indisputably marked off from the religious function, would make it far more difficult for the schools to operate. But such is obviously not the purpose of the First Amendment. That Amendment requires the state to be a neutral in its relations with groups of religious believers and nonbelievers; it does not require the state to be their adversary. State power is no more to be used so as to handicap religions than it is to favor them. . . .

The First Amendment has erected a wall between church and state. That wall must be kept high and impregnable. We could not approve the slightest breach. New Jersey has not breached it here.

Affirmed.

MR. JUSTICE JACKSON, dissenting.

I find myself, contrary to first impressions, unable to join in this decision. I have a sympathy, though it is not ideological, with Catholic citizens who are compelled by law to pay taxes for public schools, and also feel constrained by conscience and discipline to support other schools for their own children. Such relief to them as this case involves is not in itself a serious burden to taxpayers and I had assumed it to be as little serious in principle. Study of this case convinces me otherwise. The Court's opinion marshals every argument in favor of state aid and puts the case in its most favorable light, but much of its reasoning confirms my conclusions that there are no good grounds upon which to support the present legislation. In fact, the undertones of the opinion, advocating complete and uncompromising separation of Church from State, seem utterly discordant with its conclusion yielding support to their commingling in educational matters. The case which irresistibly comes to mind as the most fitting precedent is that of Julia who, according to Byron's reports, "whispering 'I will ne'er consent,'—consented."

The Township of Ewing is not furnishing transportation to the children in any form; it is not operating school buses itself or contracting for their operation; and it is not performing any public service of any kind with this taxpayer's money. All school children are left to ride as ordinary paying passengers on the regular buses operated by the public transportation system. What the Township does, and what the taxpayer complains of, is at stated intervals to reimburse parents for the fares paid, provided the children attend either public schools or Catholic Church schools. This expenditure of tax funds has no possible effect on the child's safety or expedition in transit. As passengers on the public buses they travel as fast and no faster, and are as safe and no safer, since their parents are reimbursed as before.

In addition to thus assuming a type of service that does not exist, the Court also insists that we must close our eyes to a discrimination which does exist. The resolution which authorizes disbursement of this taxpayer's money limits reimbursement to those who attend public schools and Catholic schools. That is the way the Act is applied to this taxpayer.

The New Jersey Act in question makes the character of the school, not the needs of the children, determine the eligibility of parents to reimbursement. The Act permits payment for transportation to parochial schools or public schools but prohibits it to private schools operated in whole or in part for profit. Children often are sent to private schools because their parents feel that they require more individual instruction than public schools can provide, or because they are backward or defective and need special attention. If all children of the state were objects of impartial solicitude, no reason is obvious for denying transportation reimbursement to students of this class, for these often are as needy and as worthy as those who go to public or parochial schools. Refusal to reimburse those who attend such schools is understandable only in the light of a purpose to aid the schools, because the state might well abstain from aiding a profit-making private enterprise. Thus, under the Act and resolution brought to us by this case, children are classified according to the schools they attend and are to be aided if they attend the public schools or private Catholic schools, and they are not allowed to be aided if they attend private secular schools or private religious schools of other faiths. . . .

It is no exaggeration to say that the whole historic conflict in temporal policy between the Catholic Church and non-Catholics comes to a focus in their respective school policies. The Roman Catholic Church, counseled by experience in many ages and many lands and with all sorts and conditions of men, takes what, from the viewpoint of its own progress and the success of its mission, is a wise estimate of the importance of education to religion. It does not leave the individual to pick up religion by chance. It relies on early and indelible indoctrination in the faith and order of the Church by the word and example of persons consecrated to the task.

Our public school, if not a product of Protestantism, at least is more consistent with it than with the Catholic culture and scheme of values. It is a relatively recent development dating from about 1840. It is organized on the premise that secular education can be isolated from all religious teaching so that the school can inculcate all needed temporal knowledge and also maintain a strict and lofty neutrality as to religion. The assumption is that after the individual has been instructed in worldly wisdom he will be better fitted to choose his religion. Whether such a disjunction is possible, and if possible whether it is wise, are questions I need not try to answer.

I should be surprised if any Catholic would deny that the parochial school is a vital, if not the most vital, part of the Roman Catholic Church. If put to the choice, that venerable institution, I should expect, would forego its whole service for mature persons before it would give up education of the young, and it would be a wise choice. Its growth and cohesion, discipline and loyalty, spring from its schools. Catholic education is the rock on which the whole structure rests, and to render tax aid to its Church school is indistinguishable to me from rendering the same aid to the Church itself.

It is of no importance in this situation whether the beneficiary of this expenditure of tax-raised funds is primarily the parochial school and incidentally the pupil, or whether the aid is directly bestowed on the pupil with indirect benefits to the school. The state cannot maintain a Church and it can no more tax its citizens to furnish free carriage to those who attend a Church. The prohibition against establishment of religion cannot be circumvented by a subsidy, bonus or reimbursement of expense to individuals for receiving religious instruction and indoctrination. . . .

It seems to me that the basic fallacy in the Court's reasoning, which accounts for its failure to apply the principles it avows, is in ignoring the essentially religious test by which beneficiaries of this expenditure are selected. A policeman protects a Catholic, of course—but not because he is a Catholic; it is because he is a man and a member of our society. The fireman protects the Church school—but not because it is a Church school; it is because it is property, part of the assets of our society. Neither the fireman nor the policeman has to ask before he renders aid "Is this man or building identified with the Catholic Church?" But before these school authorities draw a check to reimburse for a student's fare they must ask just that question, and if the school is a Catholic one they may render aid because it is such, while if it is of any other faith or is run for profit, the help must be withheld. To consider the converse of the Court's reasoning will best disclose its fallacy. That there is no parallel between police and fire protection and this plan of reimbursement is apparent from the incongruity of the limitation of this Act if applied to police and fire service. Could we sustain an Act that said the police shall protect pupils on the way to or from public schools and Catholic schools but not while going to and coming from other schools, and firemen shall extinguish a blaze in public or Catholic school buildings but shall not put out a blaze in Protestant Church schools or private schools operated for profit? That is the true analogy to the case we have before us and I should think it pretty plain that such a scheme would not be valid. . . .

This freedom was first in the Bill of Rights because it

was first in the forefathers' minds; it was set forth in absolute terms, and its strength is it rigidity. It was intended not only to keep the states' hands out of religion, but to keep religion's hands off the state, and, above all, to keep bitter religious controversy out of public life by denying to every denomination any advantage from getting control of public policy or the public purse. Those great ends I cannot but think are immeasurably compromised by today's decision. . . .

But we cannot have it both ways. Religious teaching cannot be a private affair when the state seeks to impose regulations which infringe on it indirectly, and a public affair when it comes to taxing citizens of one faith to aid another, or those of no faith to aid all. If these principles seem harsh in prohibiting aid to Catholic education, it must not be forgotten that it is the same Constitution that alone assures Catholics the right to maintain these schools at all when predominant local sentiment would forbid them. *Pierce* v. *Society of Sisters,* 268 U.S. 510. Nor should I think that those who have done so well without this aid would want to see this separation between Church and State broken down. If the state may aid these religious schools, it may therefore regulate them. Many groups have sought aid from tax funds only to find that it carried political controls with it.

MR. JUSTICE FRANKFURTER joins in this opinion.

MR. JUSTICE RUTLEDGE, with whom MR. JUSTICE FRANKFURTER, MR. JUSTICE JACKSON and MR. JUSTICE BURTON agree, dissenting.

Not simply an established church, but any law respecting an establishment of religion is forbidden. The Amendment was broadly but not loosely phrased. It is the compact and exact summation of its author's views formed during his long struggle for religious freedom. In Madison's own words characterizing Jefferson's Bill for Establishing Religious Freedom, the guaranty he put in our national charter, like the bill he piloted through the

Virginia Assembly, was "a Model of technical precision, and perspicuous brevity." Madison could not have confused "church" and "religion," or "an established church" and "an establishment of religion."

The Amendment's purpose was not to strike merely at the official establishment of a single sect, creed or religion, outlawing only a formal relation such as had prevailed in England and some of the colonies. Necessarily it was to uproot all such relationships. But the object was broader than separating church and state in this narrow sense. It was to create a complete and permanent separation of the spheres of religious activity and civil authority by comprehensively forbidding every form of public aid or support for religion. In proof the Amendment's wording and history unite with this Court's consistent utterances whenever attention has been fixed directly upon the question. . . .

No provision of the Constitution is more closely tied to or given content by its generating history than the religious clause of the First Amendment. It is at once the refined product and the terse summation of that history. The history includes not only Madison's authorship and the proceedings before the First Congress, but also the long and intensive struggle for religious freedom in America, more especially in Virginia, of which the Amendment was the direct culmination. In the documents of the times, particularly of Madison, who was leader in the Virginia struggle before he became the Amendment's sponsor, but also in the writings of Jefferson and others and in the issues which engendered them is to be found irrefutable confirmation of the Amendment's sweeping content.

For Madison, as also for Jefferson, religious freedom was the crux of the struggle for freedom in general. . . . Madison was co-author with George Mason of the religious clause in Virginia's great Declaration of Rights of 1776. He is credited with changing it from a mere statement of the principle of tolerance to the first official legislative pronouncement that freedom of conscience and religion are inherent rights of the individual. He sought also to have the Declaration expressly condemn the existing Virginia establishment. But the forces supporting it were then too strong.

Accordingly Madison yielded on this phase but not for long. At once he resumed the fight, continuing it before succeeding legislative sessions. As a member of the General Assembly in 1779 he threw his full weight behind Jefferson's historic Bill for Establishing Religious Freedom. That bill was a prime phase of Jefferson's broad program of democratic reform undertaken on his return from the Continental Congress in 1776 and submitted for the General Assembly's consideration in 1779 as his proposed revised Virginia code. With Jefferson's departure for Europe in 1784, Madison became the Bill's prime sponsor. Enactment failed in successive legislatures from its introduction in June, 1779, until its adoption in January, 1786. But during all this time the fight for religious freedom moved forward in Virginia on various fronts with growing intensity. Madison led throughout, against Patrick Henry's powerful opposing leadership until Henry was elected governor in November, 1784.

The climax came in the legislative struggle of 1784-1785 over the Assessment Bill. . . . This was nothing more nor less than a taxing measure for the support of religion, designed to revive the payment of tithes suspended since 1777. So long as it singled out a particular sect for preference it incurred the active and general hostility of dissentient groups. It was broadened to include them, with the result that some subsided temporarily in their opposition. As altered, the bill gave to each taxpayer the privilege of designating which church should receive his share of the tax. In default of designation the legislature applied it to pious uses. But what is of the utmost significance here, "in its final form the bill left the taxpayer the option of giving his tax to education."

Madison was unyielding at all times, opposing with all his vigor the general and nondiscriminatory as he had the earlier particular and discriminatory assessments proposed. The modified Assessment Bill passed second reading in December, 1784, and was all but enacted. Madison and his followers, however, maneuvered deferment of final consideration until November, 1785. And before the Assembly reconvened in the fall he issued his historic Memorial and Remonstrance.

This is Madison's complete, though not his only, interpretation of religious liberty. It is a broadside attack upon all forms of "establishment" of religion, both general and particular, nondiscriminatory or selective. Reflecting not only the many legislative conflicts over the Assessment Bill and the Bill for Establishing Religious Freedom but also, for example, the struggles for religious incorporations and the continued maintenance of the glebes, the Remonstrance is at once the most concise and the most accurate statement of the views of the First Amendment's author concerning what is "an establishment of religion." Because it behooves us in the dimming distance of time not to lose sight of what he and his coworkers had in mind when, by a single sweeping stroke of the pen, they forbade an establishment of religion and secured its free exercise, the text of the Remonstrance is appended at the end of this opinion for its wider current reference, together with a copy of the bill against which it was directed. [The Remonstrance and the bill are not included in this volume.]

The Remonstrance, stirring up a storm of popular protest, killed the Assessment Bill. It collapsed in committee shortly before Christmas, 1785. With this, the way was cleared at last for enactment of Jefferson's Bill for Establishing Religious Freedom. Madison promptly drove it through in January of 1786, seven years from the time it was first introduced. This dual victory substantially ended the fight over establishments, settling the issue against them. . . .

The next year Madison became a member of the Constitutional Convention. Its work done, he fought valiantly to secure the ratification of its great product in Virginia as elsewhere, and nowhere else more effectively. Madison was certain in his own mind that under the Constitution "there is not a shadow of right in the general government to intermeddle with religion" and that "this subject is, for the honor of America, perfectly free and unshackled. The government has no jurisdiction over it." Nevertheless he pledged that he would work for a Bill of Rights, including a specific guaranty of religious freedom, and Virginia, with other states, ratified the Constitution on this assurance.

Ratification thus accomplished, Madison was sent to the first Congress. There he went at once about performing his pledge to establish freedom for the nation as he had done in Virginia. Within a little more than three years from his legislative victory at home he had proposed and secured the submission and ratification of the First Amendment as the first article of our Bill of Rights.

All the great instruments of the Virginia struggle for religious liberty thus became warp and woof of our constitutional tradition, not simply by the course of history, but by the common unifying force of Madison's life, thought and sponsorship. He epitomized the whole of that tradition in the Amendment's compact, but nonetheless comprehensive, phrasing.

As the Remonstrance discloses throughout, Madison opposed every form and degree of official relation between religion and civil authority. For him religion was a wholly private matter beyond the scope of civil power either to restrain or to support. Denial or abridgment of religious freedom was a violation of rights both of conscience and of natural equality. State aid was no less obnoxious or destructive to freedom and to religion itself than other forms of state interference. "Establishment" and "free exercise" were correlative and coextensive ideas, representing only different facets of the single great and fundamental freedom. The Remonstrance, following the Virginia statute's example, referred to the history of religious conflicts and the effects of all sorts of establishments, current and historical, to suppress religion's free exercise. With Jefferson, Madison believed that to tolerate any fragment of establishment would be by so much to perpetuate restraint upon that freedom. Hence he sought to tear out the institution not partially but root and branch, and to bar its return forever.

In no phase was he more unrelentingly absolute than in opposing state support or aid by taxation. Not even "three pence" contribution was thus to be exacted from any citizen for such a purpose. . . .

In view of this history no further proof is needed that the Amendment forbids any appropriation, large or small, from public funds to aid or support any and all religious exercises. But if more were called for, the debates in the First Congress and this Court's consistent expressions, whenever it has touched on the matter directly, supply it. . . .

Does New Jersey's action furnish support for religion by use of the taxing power? Certainly it does, if the test remains undiluted as Jefferson and Madison made it, that money taken by taxation from one is not to be used or given to support another's religious training or belief, or indeed one's own. Today as then the furnishing of "contributions of money for the propagation of opinions which he disbelieves" is the forbidden exaction; and the prohibition is absolute for whatever amount may be sought or given to that end.

The funds used here were raised by taxation. The Court does not dispute, nor could it, that their use does in fact give aid and encouragement to religious instruction. It only concludes that this aid is not "support" in law. But Madison and Jefferson were concerned with aid and support in fact, not as a legal conclusion "entangled in precedents." Remonstrance, Par. 3. Here parents pay money to send their children to parochial schools and funds raised by taxation are used to reimburse them. This not only helps the children to get to school and the parents to send them. It aids them in a substantial way to get the very thing which they are sent to the particular school to secure, namely, religious training and teaching. . . .

Finally, transportation, where it is needed, is as essential to education as any other element. Its cost is as much a part of the total expense, except at times in amount, as the cost of textbooks, of school lunches, of athletic equipment, of writing and other materials; indeed of all other items composing the total burden. Now as always the core of the educational process is the teacher-pupil relationship. Without this the richest equipment and facilities would go for naught. . . . But the proverbial Mark Hopkins conception no longer suffices for the country's requirements. Without buildings, without equipment, without library, textbooks and other materials, and without transportation to bring teacher and pupil together in such an effective teaching environment, there can be not even the skeleton of what our times require. Hardly can it be maintained that transportation is the least essential of these items, or that it does not in fact aid, encourage, sustain and support, just as they do, the very process which is its purpose to accomplish. No less essential is it, or the payment of its cost, than the very teaching in the classroom or payment of the teacher's sustenance. Many types of equipment, now considered essential, better could be done without.

For me, therefore, the feat is impossible to select so indispensable an item from the composite of total costs, and characterize it as not aiding, contributing to, promoting or sustaining the propagation of beliefs which it is the very end of all to bring about. Unless this can be maintained, and the Court does not maintain it, the aid thus given is outlawed. Payment of transportation is no more, nor is it any the less essential to education, whether religious or secular, than payment for tuitions, for teachers' salaries, for buildings, equipment and necessary materials. Nor is it any the less directly related, in a school giving religious instruction, to the primary religious objective all those essential items of cost are intended to achieve. No rational line can be drawn between payment for such larger, but not more necessary, items and payment for transportation. The only line that can be so drawn is one between more dollars and less. Certainly in this realm such a line can be no valid constitutional measure. . . .

But we are told that the New Jersey statute is valid

in its present application because the appropriation is for a public, not a private purpose, namely, the promotion of education, and the majority accept this idea in the conclusion that all we have here is "public welfare legislation."

If the fact alone be determinative that religious schools are engaged in education, thus promoting the general and individual welfare, together with the legislature's decision that the payment of public moneys for their aid makes their work a public function, then I can see no possible basis, except one of dubious legislative policy, for the state's refusal to make full appropriation for support of private, religious schools, just as is done for public instruction. There could not be, on that basis, valid constitutional objection.

Of course paying the cost of transportation promotes the general cause of education and the welfare of the individual. So does paying all other items of educational expense. And obviously, as the majority say, it is much too late to urge that legislation designed to facilitate the opportunities of children to secure a secular education serves no public purpose. Our nationwide system of public education rests on the contrary view, as do all grants in aid of education, public or private, which is not religious in character. . . .

No one conscious of religious values can be unsympathetic toward the burden which our constitutional separation puts on parents who desire religious instruction mixed with secular for their children. They pay taxes for others' children's education, at the same time the added cost of instruction for their own. Nor can one happily see benefits denied to children which others receive, because in conscience they or their parents for them desire a different kind of training others do not demand.

But if those feelings should prevail, there would be an end to our historic constitutional policy and command. No more unjust or discriminatory in fact is it to deny attendants at religious schools the cost of their transportation than it is to deny them tuitions, sustenance for their teachers, or any other educational expense which others receive at public cost. Hardship in fact there is which none can blink. But, for assuring to those who undergo it the greater, the most comprehensive freedom, it is one written by design and firm intent into our basic law.

Of course discrimination in the legal sense does not exist. The child attending the religious school has the same right as any other to attend the public school. But he foregoes exercising it because the same guaranty which assures this freedom forbids the public school or any agency of the state to give or aid him in securing the religious instruction he seeks.

Were he to accept the common school, he would be the first to protest the teaching there of any creed or faith not his own. And it is precisely for the reason that their atmosphere is wholly secular that children are not sent to public schools under the *Pierce* doctrine. But that is a constitutional necessity, because we have staked the very existence of our country on the faith that complete separation between the state and religion is best for the state and best for religion. Remonstrance, Par. 8, 12.

That policy necessarily entails hardship upon persons who forego the right to educational advantages the state can supply in order to secure others it is precluded from giving. Indeed this may hamper the parent and the child forced by conscience to that choice. But it does not make the state unneutral to withhold what the Constitution forbids it to give. On the contrary it is only by observing the prohibition rigidly that the state can maintain its neutrality and avoid partisanship in the dissensions inevitable when sect opposes sect over demands for public moneys to further religious education, teaching or training in any form or degree, directly or indirectly. Like St. Paul's freedom, religious liberty with a great price must be bought. And for those who exercise it most fully, by insisting upon religious education for their children mixed with secular, by the terms of our Constitution the price is greater than for others.

The problem then cannot be cast in terms of legal discrimination or its absence. This would be true, even though the state in giving aid should treat all religious instruction alike. Thus, if the present statute and its application were shown to apply equally to all religious schools of whatever faith, yet in the light of our tradition it could not stand. For then the adherent of one creed still would pay for the support of another, the childless taxpayer with others more fortunate. Then too there would seem to be no bar to making appropriations for transportation and other expenses of children attending public or other secular schools, after hours in separate places and classes for their exclusively religious instruction. The person who embraces no creed also would be forced to pay for teaching what he does not believe. Again, it was the furnishing of "contributions of money for the propagation of opinions which he disbelieves" that the fathers outlawed. That consequence and effect are not removed by multiplying to all-inclusiveness the sects for which support is exacted. The Constitution requires, not comprehensive identification of state with religion, but complete separation. . . .

4

West Virginia State Board of Education v. Barnette

319 U.S. 624 (1943)

In 1940, in Minersville School District v. *Gobitis, 310 U.S. 586, the Supreme Court held that "the promotion of national cohesion" through the compulsory flag salute in the public schools is a more important interest than that of religious freedom. Mr. Justice Stone stood alone in dissenting from this decision. When the question came up again in 1943, the Court reversed itself, and ruled the other way by a five-to-three vote. Portions of the majority and dissenting opinions are given below; two other concurring opinions were also written.*

MR. JUSTICE JACKSON delivered the opinion of the Court.

Following the decision by this Court on June 3, 1940, in *Minersville School District* v. *Gobitis,* 310 U.S. 586, the West Virginia legislature amended its statutes to require all schools therein to conduct courses of instruction in history, civics, and in the Constitutions of the United States and of the State "for the purpose of teaching, fostering and perpetuating the ideals, principles and spirit of Americanism, and increasing the knowledge of the organization and machinery of the government." Appellant Board of Education was directed, with advice of the State Superintendent of Schools, to "prescribe the courses of study covering these subjects" for public schools. The Act made it the duty of private, parochial and denominational schools to prescribe courses of study "similar to those required for the public schools."

The Board of Education on January 9, 1942, adopted a resolution containing recitals taken largely from the Court's *Gobitis* opinion and ordering that the salute to the flag become "a regular part of the program of activities in the public schools," that all teachers and pupils "shall be required to participate in the salute honoring the Nation represented by the Flag; provided, however, that refusal to salute the Flag be regarded as an act of insubordination, and shall be dealt with accordingly."

The resolution originally required the "commonly accepted salute to the Flag" which it defined. Objections to the salute as "being too much like Hitler's" were raised by the Parent and Teachers Association, the Boy and Girl Scouts, the Red Cross, and the Federation of Women's Clubs. Some modification appears to have been made in deference to these objections, but no concession was made to Jehovah's Witnesses. What is now required is the "stiff-arm" salute, the saluter to keep the right hand raised with palm turned up while the following is repeated: "I pledge allegiance to the Flag of the United States of America and to the Republic for which it stands; one Nation, indivisible, with liberty and justice for all."

Failure to conform is "insubordination" dealt with by expulsion. Readmission is denied by statute until compliance. Meanwhile the expelled child is "unlawfully absent" and may be proceeded against as a delinquent. His parents or guardians are liable to prosecution, and if convicted are subject to fine not exceeding $50 and jail term not exceeding thirty days.

Appellees, citizens of the United States and of West Virginia, brought suit in the United States District Court for themselves and others similarly situated asking its injunction to restrain enforcement of these laws and regulations against Jehovah's Witnesses. The Witnesses are an unincorporated body teaching that the obligation imposed by law of God is superior to that of laws enacted by temporal government. Their religious beliefs include a literal version of Exodus, Chapter 20, verses 4 and 5, which says: "Thou shalt not make unto thee any graven image, or any likeness of anything that is in heaven above, or that is in the earth beneath, or that is in the water under the earth; thou shalt not bow down thyself to them nor serve them." They consider that the flag is an "image" within this command. For this reason they refuse to salute it.

Children of this faith have been expelled from school and are threatened with exclusion for no other cause. Officials threaten to send them to reformatories maintained for criminally inclined juveniles. Parents of such children have been prosecuted and are threatened with prosecutions for causing delinquency.

The Board of Education moved to dismiss the complaint setting forth these facts and alleging that the law and regulations are an unconstitutional denial of religious freedom, and of freedom of speech, and are invalid under the "due process" and "equal protection" clauses of the Fourteenth Amendment to the Federal Constitution. The cause was submitted on the pleadings to a District Court of three judges. It restrained enforcement as to the plaintiffs and those of that class. The Board of Education brought the case here by direct appeal.

This case calls upon us to reconsider a precedent decision, as the Court throughout its history often has been required to do. Before turning to the *Gobitis* case, however, it is desirable to notice certain characteristics by which this controversy is distinguished.

The freedom asserted by these appellees does not bring them into collision with rights asserted by any other individual. It is such conflicts which most frequently require intervention of the State to determine where the rights of one end and those of another begin. But the refusal of these persons to participate in the ceremony does not interfere with or deny rights of others to do so. Nor is there any question in this case that their behavior is peaceable and orderly. The sole conflict is between authority and rights of the individual. The State asserts power to condition access to public education on making a prescribed sign and profession and at the same time to coerce attendance by punishing both parent and child. The latter stand on a right of self-determination in matters that touch individual opinion and personal attitude. . . .

There is no doubt that, in connection with the pledges, the flag salute is a form of utterance. Symbolism is a primitive but effective way of communicating ideas. The use of an emblem or flag to symbolize some system, idea, institution, or personality, is a short cut from mind to mind. Causes and nations, political parties, lodges and ecclesiastical groups seek to knit the loyalty of their followings to a flag or banner, a color or design. The State announces rank, function, and authority through crowns and maces, uniforms and black robes; the church speaks through the Cross, the Crucifix, the altar and shrine, and clerical raiment. Symbols of State often convey political ideas just as religious symbols come to convey theological ones. Associated with many of these symbols are appropriate gestures of acceptance or respect: a salute, a bowed or bared head, a bended knee. A person gets from a symbol the meaning he puts into it, and what is one man's comfort and inspiration is another's jest and scorn. . . .

It is also to be noted that the compulsory flag salute and pledge requires affirmation of a belief and an attitude of mind. It is not clear whether the regulation contemplates that pupils forego any contrary convictions of their own and become unwilling converts to the prescribed ceremony or whether it will be acceptable if they simulate assent by words without belief and by a gesture barren of meaning. It is now a commonplace that censorship or suppression of expression of opinion is tolerated by our Constitution only when the expression presents a clear and present danger of action of a kind the State is empowered to prevent and punish. It would seem that involuntary affirmation could be commanded only on even more immediate and urgent grounds than silence. But here the power of compulsion is invoked without any allegation that remaining passive during a flag salute ritual creates a clear and present danger that would justify an effort even to muffle expression. To sustain the compulsory flag salute we are required to say that a Bill of Rights which guards the individual's right to speak his own mind, left it open to public authorities to compel him to utter what is not in his mind.

Whether the First Amendment to the Constitution will permit officials to order observance of ritual of this nature does not depend upon whether as a voluntary exercise we would think it to be good, bad or merely innocuous. Any credo of nationalism is likely to include what some disapprove or to omit what others think essential, and to give off different overtones as it takes on different accents or interpretations. If official power exists to coerce acceptance of any patriotic creed, what it shall contain cannot be decided by courts, but must be largely discretionary with the ordaining authority, whose power to prescribe would no doubt include power to amend. Hence validity of the asserted power to force an American citizen publicly to profess any statement of belief or to engage in any ceremony of assent to one, presents questions of power that must be considered independently of any idea we may have as to the utility of the ceremony in question.

Nor does the issue as we see it turn on one's possession of particular religious views or the sincerity with which they are held. While religion supplies appellees' motive for enduring the discomforts of making the issue in this case, many citizens who do not share these religious views hold such a compulsory rite to infringe constitutional liberty of the individual. It is not necessary to inquire whether nonconformist beliefs will exempt from the duty to salute unless we first find power to make the salute a legal duty.

The *Gobitis* decision, however, *assumed,* as did the argument in that case and in this, that power exists in the State to impose the flag salute discipline upon school children in general. The Court only examined and rejected a claim based on religious beliefs of immunity from an unquestioned general rule. The question which underlies the flag salute controversy is whether such a ceremony so touching matters of opinion and political attitude may be imposed upon the individual by official authority under powers committed to any political organization under our Constitution. We examine rather than assume existence of this power and, against this broader definition of issues in this case, reexamine specific grounds assigned for the *Gobitis* decision.

1. It was said that the flag-salute controversy con-

fronted the Court with "the problem which Lincoln cast in memorable dilemma: 'Must a government of necessity be too *strong* for the liberties of its people, or too *weak* to maintain its own existence?'" and that the answer must be in favor of strength. . . .

We think these issues may be examined free of pressure or restraint growing out of such considerations.

It may be doubted whether Mr. Lincoln would have thought that the strength of government to maintain itself would be impressively vindicated by our confirming power of the State to expel a handful of children from school. Such oversimplification, so handy in political debate, often lacks the precision necessary to postulates of judicial reasoning. If validly applied to this problem, the utterance cited would resolve every issue of power in favor of those in authority and would require us to override every liberty thought to weaken or delay execution of their policies.

Government of limited power need not be anemic government. Assurance that rights are secure tends to diminish fear and jealousy of strong government, and by making us feel safe to live under it makes for its better support. Without promise of a limiting Bill of Rights it is doubtful if our Constitution could have mustered enough strength to enable its ratification. To enforce those rights today is not to choose weak government over strong government. It is only to adhere as a means of strength to individual freedom of mind in preference to officially disciplined uniformity for which history indicates a disappointing and disastrous end.

The subject now before us exemplifies this principle. Free public education, if faithful to the ideal of secular instruction and political neutrality, will not be partisan or enemy of any class, creed, party, or faction. If it is to impose any ideological discipline, however, each party or denomination must seek to control, or failing that, to weaken the influence of the educational system. Observance of the limitations of the Constitution will not weaken government in the field appropriate for its exercise.

2. It was also considered in the *Gobitis* case that functions of educational officers in States, counties and school districts were such that to interfere with their authority "would in effect make us the school board for the country."

The Fourteenth Amendment, as now applied to the States, protects the citizen against the State itself and all of its creatures—Boards of Education not excepted. These have, of course, important, delicate, and highly discretionary functions, but none that they may not perform within the limits of the Bill of Rights. That they are educating the young for citizenship is reason for scrupulous protection of Constitutional freedoms of the individual, if we are not to strangle the free mind at its source and teach youth to discount important principles of our government as mere platitudes.

Such Boards are numerous and their territorial jurisdiction often small. But small and local authority may feel less sense of responsibility to the Constitution, and agencies of publicity may be less vigilant in calling it to account. The action of Congress in making flag observance voluntary and respecting the conscience of the objector in a matter so vital as raising the Army contrasts sharply with these local regulations in matters relatively trivial to the welfare of the nation. There are village tyrants as well as village Hampdens, but none who acts under color of law is beyond reach of the Constitution.

3. The *Gobitis* opinion reasoned that this is a field "where courts possess no marked and certainly no controlling competence," that it is committed to the legislatures as well as the courts to guard cherished liberties and that it is constitutionally appropriate to "fight out the wise use of legislative authority in the forum of public opinion and before legislative assemblies rather than to transfer such a contest to the judicial arena," since all the "effective means of inducing political changes are left free."

The very purpose of a Bill of Rights was to withdraw certain subjects from the vicissitudes of political controversy, to place them beyond the reach of majorities and officials and to establish them as legal principles to be applied by the courts. One's right to life, liberty, and property, to free speech, a free press, freedom of worship and assembly, and other fundamental rights may not be submitted to vote; they depend on the outcome of no elections.

In weighing arguments of the parties it is important to distinguish between the due process clause of the Fourteenth Amendment as an instrument for transmitting the principles of the First Amendment and those cases in which it is applied for its own sake. The test of legislation which collides with the Fourteenth Amendment, because it also collides with the principles of the First, is much more definite than the test when only the Fourteenth is involved. Much of the vagueness of the due process clause disappears when the specific prohibitions of the First become its standard. The right of a State to regulate, for example, a public utility may well include, so far as the due process test is concerned, power to impose all of the restrictions which a legislature may have a "rational basis" for adopting. But freedoms of speech and of press, of assembly, and of worship may not be infringed on such slender grounds. They are susceptible of restriction only to prevent grave and immediate danger to interests which the State may lawfully protect. It is important to note that while it is the Fourteenth Amendment which bears directly upon the State it is the more specific limiting principles of the First Amendment that finally govern this case.

Nor does our duty to apply the Bill of Rights to assertions of official authority depend upon our possession of marked competence in the field where the invasion of rights occurs. True, the task of translating the majestic generalities of the Bill of Rights, conceived as part of the pattern of liberal government in the eighteenth century, into concrete restraints on officials dealing with the problems of the twentieth century, is one to disturb self-confidence. These principles grew in soil which also produced a philosophy that the individual was the center of society, that his liberty was attainable through mere absence of governmental restraints, and that government should be entrusted with few controls and only the mildest supervision over men's affairs. We must transplant these rights to a soil in which the *laissez-faire* concept or principle of noninterference has withered at least as to economic affairs, and social advancements are increasingly sought through closer integration of society and through expanded and strengthened governmental controls. These changed conditions often deprive precedents of reliability and cast us more than we would choose upon our own judgment. But we act in these matters not by authority of our competence but by force of our commissions. We cannot, because of modest estimates of our competence in such specialties as public education, withhold the judgment that history authenticates as the function of this Court when liberty is infringed.

4. Lastly, and this is the very heart of the *Gobitis* opinion, it reasons that "National unity is the basis of national security," that the authorities have "the right to select appropriate means for its attainment," and hence reaches the conclusion that such compulsory measures toward "national unity" are constitutional. Upon the verity of this assumption depends our answer in this case.

National unity as an end which officials may foster by persuasion and example is not in question. The problem is whether under our Constitution compulsion as here employed is a permissible means for its achievement.

Struggles to coerce uniformity of sentiment in support of some end thought essential to their time and country have been waged by many good as well as by evil men. Nationalism is a relatively recent phenomenon but at other times and places the ends have been racial or territorial security, support of a dynasty or regime, and particular plans for saving souls. As first and moderate methods to attain unity have failed, those bent on its accomplishment must resort to an ever-increasing severity. As governmental pressure toward unity becomes greater, so strife becomes more bitter as to whose unity it shall be. Probably no deeper division of our people could proceed from any provocation than from finding it necessary to choose what doctrine and whose program public educational officials shall compel youth to unite in embracing. Ultimate futility of such attempts to compel coherence is the lesson of every such effort from the Roman drive to stamp out Christianity as a disturber of its pagan unity, the Inquisition, as a means to religious and dynastic unity, the Siberian exiles as a means to Russian unity, down to the fast failing efforts of our present totalitarian enemies. Those who begin coercive elimination of dissent soon find themselves exterminating dissenters. Compulsory unification of opinion achieves only the unanimity of the graveyard.

It seems trite but necessary to say that the First Amendment to our Constitution was designed to avoid these ends by avoiding these beginnings. There is no mysticism in the American concept of the State or of the nature or origin of its authority. We set up government by consent of the governed, and the Bill of Rights denies those in power any legal opportunity to coerce that consent. Authority here is to be controlled by public opinion, not public opinion by authority.

The case is made difficult not because the principles of its decision are obscure but because the flag involved is our own. Nevertheless, we apply the limitations of the Constitution with no fear that freedom to be intellectually and spiritually diverse or even contrary will disintegrate the social organization. To believe that patriotism will not flourish if patriotic ceremonies are voluntary and spontaneous instead of a compulsory routine is to make an unflattering estimate of the appeal of our institutions to free minds. We can have intellectual individualism and the rich cultural diversities that we owe to exceptional minds only at the price of occasional eccentricity and abnormal attitudes. When they are so harmless to others or to the State as those we deal with here, the price is not too great. But freedom to differ is not limited to things that do not matter much. That would be a mere shadow of freedom. The test of its substance is the right to differ as to things that touch the heart of the existing order.

If there is any fixed star in our constitutional constellation, it is that no official, high or petty, can prescribe what shall be orthodox in politics, nationalism, religion, or other matters of opinion or force citizens to confess by word or act their faith therein. If there are any circumstances which permit an exception, they do not now occur to us. . . .

The decision of this Court in *Minersville School District* v. *Gobitis* and the holdings of those few *per curiam* decisions which preceded and foreshadowed it are overruled, and the judgment enjoining enforcement of the West Virginia Regulation is *affirmed*. . . .

MR. JUSTICE FRANKFURTER, dissenting.

One who belongs to the most vilified and persecuted minority in history is not likely to be insensible to the freedoms guaranteed by our Constitution. Were my purely personal attitude relevant I should wholeheartedly associate myself with the general libertarian views in the Court's opinion, representing as they do the thought and action of a lifetime. But as judges we are neither Jew nor Gentile, neither Catholic nor agnostic. We owe equal attachment to the Constitution and are equally bound by our judicial obligations whether we derive our citizenship from the earliest or the latest immigrants to these shores. As a member of this Court I am not justified in writing my private notions of policy into the Constitution, no matter how deeply I may cherish them or how mischievous I may deem their disregard. The duty of a judge who must decide which of two claims before the Court shall prevail, that of a State to enact and enforce laws within its general competence or that of an individual to refuse obedience because of the demands of his conscience, is not that of the ordinary person. It can never be emphasized too much that one's own opinion about the wisdom or evil of a law should be excluded altogether when one is doing one's duty on the bench. The only opinion of our own even looking in that direction that is material is our opinion whether legislators could in reason have enacted such a law. In the light of all the circumstances, including the history of this question in this Court, it would require more daring than I possess to deny that reasonable legislators could have taken the action which is before us for review. Most unwillingly, therefore, I must differ from my brethren with regard to legislation like this. I cannot bring my mind to believe that the "liberty" secured by the Due Process Clause gives this Court authority to deny to the State of West Virginia the attainment of that which we all recognize as a legitimate legislative end, namely, the promotion of good citizenship, by employment of the means here chosen. . . .

We are not reviewing merely the action of a local school board. The flag salute requirement in this case comes before us with the full authority of the State of West Virginia. We are in fact passing judgment on "the power of the State as a whole." . . . Practically we are passing upon the political power of each of the forty-eight states. . . .

The constitutional protection of religious freedom terminated disabilities, it did not create new privileges. It gave religious equality, not civil immunity. Its essence is freedom from conformity to religious dogma, not freedom from conformity to law because of religious dogma. Religious loyalties may be exercised without hindrance from the state, not the state may not exercise that which except by leave of religious loyalties is within the domain of temporal power. Otherwise each individual could set up his own censor against obedience to laws conscientiously deemed for the public good by those whose business it is to make laws. . . .

An act compelling profession of allegiance to a religion, no matter how subtly or tenuously promoted, is bad. But an act promoting good citizenship and national allegiance is within the domain of governmental authority and is therefore to be judged by the same considerations of power and of constitutionality as those involved in the many claims of immunity from civil obedience because of religious scruples.

That claims are pressed on behalf of sincere religious convictions does not of itself establish their constitutional validity. Nor does waving the banner of religious freedom relieve us from examining into the power we are asked to deny the states. Otherwise the doctrine of separation of church and state, so cardinal in the history of this nation and for the liberty of the people, would mean not the disestablishment of a state church but the establishment of all churches and of all religious groups. . . .

We are told that symbolism is a dramatic but primitive way of communicating ideas. Symbolism is inescapable. Even the most sophisticated live by symbols. But it is not for this Court to make psychological judgments as to the effectiveness of a particular symbol in inculcating concededly indispensable feelings, particularly if the state happens to see fit to utilize the symbol that represents our heritage and our hopes. And surely only flippancy could be responsible for the suggestion that constitutional validity of a requirement to salute our flag implies equal validity of a requirement to salute a dictator. The significance of a symbol lies in what it represents. To reject the swastika does not imply rejection of the Cross. And so it bears repetition to say that it mocks reason and denies our whole history to find in the allowance of a requirement to salute our flag on fitting occasions the seeds of sanction for obeisance to a leader. To deny the power to employ educational symbols is to say that the state's educational system may not stimulate the imagination because this may lead to unwise stimulation. . . .

Of course patriotism cannot be enforced by the flag salute. But neither can the liberal spirit be enforced by judicial invalidation of illiberal legislation. Our constant preoccupation with the constitutionality of legislation rather than with its wisdom tends to preoccupation of the American mind with a false value. The tendency of focusing attention on constitutionality is to make constitutionality synonymous with wisdom, to regard a law as all right if it is constitutional. Such an attitude is a great enemy of liberalism. Particularly in legislation affecting freedom of thought and freedom of speech much which should offend a free-spirited society is constitutional. Reliance for the most precious interests of civilization, therefore, must be found outside of their vindication in courts of law. Only a persistent positive translation of the faith of a free society into the convictions and habits and actions of a community is the ultimate reliance against unabated temptations to fetter the human spirit.

5

Illinois ex rel. McCollum v. Board of Education

333 U.S. 203 (1948)

Appeal from the Supreme Court of Illinois.

MR. JUSTICE BLACK delivered the opinion of the Court.

This case relates to the power of a state to utilize its tax-supported public school system in aid of religious instruction insofar as that power may be restricted by the First and Fourteenth Amendments to the Federal Constitution.

The appellant, Vashti McCollum, began this action for mandamus against the Champaign Board of Education in the Circuit Court of Champaign County, Illinois. Her asserted interest was that of a resident and taxpayer of Champaign and of a parent whose child was then enrolled in the Champaign public schools. Illinois has a compulsory education law which, with exceptions, requires parents to send their children, aged seven to sixteen, to its tax-supported public schools where the children are to remain in attendance during the hours when the schools are regularly in session. Parents who violate this law commit a misdemeanor punishable by fine unless the children attend private or parochial schools which meet educational standards fixed by the State. District boards of education are given general supervisory powers over the use of the public school buildings within the school districts. . . .

Appellant's petition for mandamus alleged that religious teachers, employed by private religious groups, were permitted to come weekly into the school buildings during the regular hours set apart for secular teaching, and then and there for a period of thirty minutes substitute their religious teaching for the secular education provided under the compulsory education law. The petitioner charged that this joint public-school religious-group program violated the First and Fourteenth Amendments to the United States Constitution. . . .

Although there are disputes between the parties as to various inferences that may or may not properly be drawn from the evidence concerning the religious program, the following facts are shown by the record without dispute. In 1940 interested members of the Jewish, Roman Catholic, and a few of the Protestant faiths formed a voluntary association called the Champaign Council on Religious Education. They obtained permission from the Board of Education to offer classes in religious instruction to public school pupils in grades four to nine inclusive. Classes were made up of pupils whose parents signed printed cards requesting that their children be permitted to attend; they were held weekly, thirty minutes for the lower grades, forty-five minutes for the higher. The council employed the religious teachers at no expense to the school authorities, but the instructors were subject to the approval and supervision of the superintendent of schools. The classes were taught in three separate religious groups by Protestant teachers, Catholic priests, and a Jewish rabbi, although for the past several years there have apparently been no classes instructed in the Jewish religion. Classes were conducted in the regular classrooms of the school building. Students who did not choose to take the religious instruction were not released from public school duties; they were required to leave their classrooms and go to some other place in the school building for pursuit of their secular studies. On the other hand, students who were released from secular study for the religious instructions were required to be present at the religious classes. Reports of their presence or absence were to be made to their secular teachers.

The foregoing facts, without reference to others that appear in the record, show the use of tax-supported property for religious instruction and the close cooperation between the school authorities and the religious council in promoting religious education. The operation of the State's compulsory education system thus assists and is integrated with the program of religious instruction carried on by separate religious sects. Pupils compelled by law to go to school for secular education are released in part from their legal duty upon the condition that they attend the religious classes. This is beyond all question a utilization of the tax-established and tax-supported public school system to aid religious groups to spread their faith. And it falls squarely under the ban of the First Amendment (made applicable to the States by the Fourteenth) as we interpreted it in *Everson* v. *Board of Education,* 330 U.S. 1. . . .

Recognizing that the Illinois program is barred by the First and Fourteenth Amendments if we adhere to the views expressed both by the majority and the minority in the *Everson* case, counsel for the respondents challenge those views as dicta and urge that we reconsider and repudiate them. They argue that historically the First Amendment was intended to forbid only government preference of one religion over another, not an impartial governmental assistance of all religions. In addition they ask that we distinguish or overrule our holding in the *Everson* case that the Fourteenth Amendment made the "establishment of religion" clause of the First Amendment applicable as a prohibition against the States. After giving full consideration to the arguments presented we are unable to accept either of these contentions.

To hold that a state cannot consistently with the First and Fourteenth Amendments utilize its public school system to aid any or all religious faiths or sects in the dissemination of their doctrines and ideals does not, as counsel urge, manifest a governmental hostility to religion or religious teachings. A manifestation of such hostility would be at war with our national tradition as embodied in the First Amendment's guaranty of the free exercise of religion. For the First Amendment rests upon the premise that both religion and government can best work to achieve their lofty aims if each is left free from the other within its respective sphere. Or, as we said in the *Everson* case, the First Amendment has erected a wall between Church and State which must be kept high and impregnable.

Here not only are the State's tax-supported public school buildings used for the dissemination of religious doctrines. The State also affords sectarian groups an invaluable aid in that it helps to provide pupils for their religious classes through use of the State's compulsory public school machinery. This is not separation of Church and State.

The cause is reversed and remanded to the State Supreme Court for proceedings not inconsistent with this opinion.

Reversed and remanded.

MR. JUSTICE FRANKFURTER delivered the following opinion, in which MR. JUSTICE JACKSON, MR. JUSTICE RUTLEDGE and MR. JUSTICE BURTON join.

We dissented in *Everson* v. *Board of Education,* 330 U. S. 1, because in our view the Constitutional principle requiring separation of Church and State compelled invalidation of the ordinance sustained by the majority. Illinois has here authorized the commingling of sectarian with secular instruction in the public schools. The Constitution of the United States forbids this.

This case, in the light of the *Everson* decision, demonstrates anew that the mere formulation of a relevant Constitutional principle is the beginning of the solution of a problem, not its answer. This is so because the meaning of a spacious conception like that of the separation of Church from State is unfolded as appeal is made to the principle from case to case. We are all agreed that the First and the Fourteenth Amendments have a secular reach far more penetrating in the conduct of Government than merely to forbid an "established church." But agreement, in the abstract, that the First Amendment was designed to erect a "wall of separation between church and State," does not preclude a clash of views as to what the wall separates. Involved is not only the Constitutional principle but the implications of judicial review in its enforcement. Accommodation of legislative freedom and Constitutional limitations upon that freedom cannot be achieved by a mere phrase. We cannot illuminatingly apply the "wall-of-separation" metaphor until we have considered the relevant history of religious education in America, the place of the "released time" movement in that history, and its precise manifestation in the case before us.

To understand the particular program now before us as a conscientious attempt to accommodate the allowable functions of Government and the special concerns of the Church within the framework of our Constitution and with due regard to the kind of society for which it was designed, we must put this Champaign program of 1940 in its historic setting. Traditionally, organized education in the Western world was Church education. It could hardly be otherwise when the education of children was primarily study of the Word and the ways of God. Even in the Protestant countries, where there was a less close identification of Church and State, the basis of education was largely the Bible, and its chief purpose inculcation of piety. To the extent that the State intervened, it used its authority to further aims of the Church.

The emigrants who came to these shores brought this view of education with them. Colonial schools certainly started with a religious orientation. When the common problems of the early settlers of the Massachusetts Bay Colony revealed the need for common schools, the object was the defeat of "one chief project of that old deluder, Satan, to keep men from the knowledge of the Scriptures." The Laws and Liberties of Massachusetts, 1648 edition (Cambridge 1929) 47.

The evolution of colonial education, largely in the service of religion, into the public school system of today is the story of changing conceptions regarding the American democratic society, of the functions of State-maintained education in such a society, and of the role therein of the free exercise of religion by the people. The modern public school derived from a philosophy of freedom reflected in the First Amendment. It is appropriate to recall that the Remonstrance of James Madison, an event basic in the history of religious liberty, was called forth by a proposal which involved support to religious education. . . . As the momentum for popular education increased and in turn evoked strong claims for State support of religious education, contests not unlike that which in Virginia had produced Madison's Remonstrance appeared in various forms in other States. New York and Massachusetts provide famous chapters in the history that established dissociation of religious teaching from State-maintained schools. In New York, the rise of the common schools led, despite fierce sectarian opposition, to the barring of tax funds to church schools, and later to any school in which sectarian doctrine was taught. In Massachusetts, largely through the efforts of Horace Mann, all sectarian teachings were barred from the common school to save it from being rent by denominational conflict. The upshot of these controversies, often long and fierce, is fairly summarized by saying that long before the Fourteenth Amendment subjected the States to new limitations, the prohibition of furtherance by the State of religious instruction became the guiding principle, in law and feeling, of the American people. . . .

Separation in the field of education, then, was not imposed upon unwilling States by force of superior law. In this respect the Fourteenth Amendment merely reflected a principle then dominant in our national life. To the extent that the Constitution thus made it binding upon the States, the basis of the restriction is the whole experience of our people. Zealous watchfulness against fusion of secular and religious activities by Government itself, through any of its instruments but especially through its educational agencies, was the democratic response of the American community to the particular needs of a young and growing nation, unique in the composition of its people. . . .

It is pertinent to remind that the establishment of this principle of Separation in the field of education was not due to any decline in the religious beliefs of the people. Horace Mann was a devout Christian, and the deep religious feeling of James Madison is stamped upon the Remonstrance. The secular public school did not imply indifference to the basic role of religion in the life of the people, nor rejection of religious education as a means of fostering it. The claims of religion were not minimized by refusing to make the public schools agencies for their assertion. The nonsectarian or secular public school was the means of reconciling freedom in general with religious freedom. The sharp confinement of the public schools to secular education was a recognition of the need of a democratic society to educate its children, insofar as the State undertook to do so, in an atmosphere free from pressures in a realm in which pressures are most resisted and where conflicts are most easily and most bitterly engendered. Designed to serve as perhaps the most powerful agency for promoting cohesion among a heterogeneous democratic people, the public school must keep scrupulously free from entanglement in the strife of sects. The preservation of the community from divisive conflicts, of Government from irreconcilable pressures by religious groups, of religion from censorship and coercion however subtly exercised, requires strict confinement of the State to instruction other than religious, leaving to the individual's church and home, indoctrination in the faith of his choice. . . .

MR. JUSTICE JACKSON, concurring.

I join the opinion of MR. Justice FRANKFURTER, and concur in the result reached by the Court, but with these reservations: I think it is doubtful whether the facts of this case establish jurisdiction in this Court, but in any event that we should place some bounds on the demands for interference with local schools that we are empowered or willing to entertain. I make these reservations a matter of record in view of the number of litigations likely to be started as a result of this decision. . . .

MR. JUSTICE REED, dissenting.

As I am convinced that this interpretation of the First Amendment is erroneous, I feel impelled to express the reasons for my disagreement. By directing attention to the many instances of close association of church and state in American society and by recalling that many of these relations are so much a part of our tradition and culture that they are accepted without more, this dissent may help in an appraisal of the meaning of the clause of the First Amendment concerning the establishment of religion and of the reasons which lead to the approval or disapproval of the judgment below. . . .

I find it difficult to extract from the opinions any conclusion as to what it is in the Champaign plan that is unconstitutional. Is it the use of school buildings for religious instruction; the release of pupils by the schools for religious instruction during school hours; the so-called assistance by teachers in handing out the request cards to pupils, in keeping lists of them for release and records of their attendance; or the action of the principals in arranging an opportunity for the classes and the appearance of the Council's instructors? None of the reversing opinions say whether the purpose of the Champaign plan for religious instruction during school hours is unconstitutional or whether it is some ingredient used in or omitted from the formula that makes the plan unconstitutional.

From the tenor of the opinions I conclude that their teachings are that any use of a pupil's school time, whether that use is on or off the school grounds, with the necessary school regulations to facilitate attendance, falls under the ban. . . .

Mr. Jefferson, as one of the founders of the University of Virginia, a school which from its establishment in 1819 has been wholly governed, managed and controlled by the State of Virginia, was faced with the same problem that is before this Court today: the question of the constitutional limitation upon religious education in public schools. In his annual report as Rector, to the President and Directors of the Literary Fund, dated October 7, 1822, approved by the Visitors of the University of whom Mr. Madison was one, Mr. Jefferson set forth his views at some length. These suggestions of Mr.

Jefferson were adopted and ch. II, § 1, of the Regulations of the University of October 4, 1824, provided that:

> Should the religious sects of this State, or any of them, according to the invitation held out to them, establish within, or adjacent to, the precincts of the University, schools for instruction in the religion of their sect, the students of the University will be free, and expected to attend religious worship at the establishment of their respective sects, in the morning, and in time to meet their school in the University at its stated hour.

Thus, the "wall of separation between church and State" that Mr. Jefferson built at the University which he founded did not exclude religious education from that school. The difference between the generality of his statements on the separation of church and state and the specificity of his conclusions on education are considerable. A rule of law should not be drawn from a figure of speech.

Mr. Madison's *Memorial and Remonstrance against Religious Assessments,* relied upon by the dissenting Justices in *Everson,* is not applicable here. Mr. Madison was one of the principal opponents in the Virginia General Assembly of A Bill Establishing a Provision for Teachers of the Christian Religion. The monies raised by the taxing section of that bill were to be appropriated "by the Vestries, Elders, or Directors of each religious society, . . . to a provision for a Minister or Teacher of the Gospel of their denomination, or the providing places of divine worship, and to none other use whatsoever. . . ." The conclusive legislative struggle over this act took place in the fall of 1785, before the adoption of the Bill of Rights. The *Remonstrance* had been issued before the General Assembly convened and was instrumental in the final defeat of the act, which died in committee. Throughout the *Remonstrance,* Mr. Madison speaks of the "establishment" sought to be effected by the act. It is clear from its historical setting and its language that the *Remonstrance* was a protest against an effort by Virginia to support Christian sects by taxation. Issues similar to those raised by the instant case were not discussed. Thus, Mr. Madison's approval of Mr. Jefferson's report as Rector gives, in my opinion, a clearer indication of his views on the constitutionality of religious education in public schools than his general statements on a different subject. . . .

It seems clear to me that the "aid" referred to by the Court in the *Everson* case could not have been those incidental advantages that religious bodies, with other groups similarly situated, obtain as a by-product of organized society. This explains the well-known fact that all churches receive "aid" from government in the form of freedom from taxation. The *Everson* decision itself justified the transportation of children to church schools by New Jersey for safety reasons. It accords with *Cochran* v. *Louisiana State Board of Education,* 281 U.S. 370, where this Court upheld a free textbook statute of Louisiana against a charge that it aided private schools on the ground that the books were for the education of the children, not to aid religious schools. Likewise the National School Lunch Act aids all school children attending tax-exempt schools. In *Bradfield* v. *Roberts,* 175 U.S. 291, this Court held proper the payment of money by the federal government to build an addition to a hospital, chartered by individuals who were members of a Roman Catholic sisterhood, and operated under the auspices of the Roman Catholic Church. This was done over the objection that it aided the establishment of religion. While obviously in these instances the respective churches, in a certain sense, were aided, this Court has never held that such "aid" was in violation of the First or Fourteenth Amendment. . . .

The practices of the federal government offer many examples of this kind of "aid" by the state to religion. The Congress of the United States has a chaplain for each House who daily invokes divine blessings and guidance for the proceedings. The armed forces have commissioned chaplains from early days. They conduct the public services in accordance with the liturgical requirements of their respective faiths, ashore and afloat, employing for the purpose property belonging to the United States and dedicated to the services of religion. Under the Servicemen's Readjustment Act of 1944, eligible veterans may receive training at government expense for the ministry in denominational schools. The schools of the District of Columbia have opening exercises which "include a reading from the Bible without note or comment, and the Lord's prayer."

In the United States Naval Academy and the United States Military Academy, schools wholly supported and completely controlled by the federal government, there are a number of religious activities. Chaplains are attached to both schools. Attendance at church services on Sunday is compulsory at both the Military and Naval Academies. At West Point the Protestant services are held in the Cadet Chapel, the Catholic in the Catholic Chapel, and the Jewish in the Old Cadet Chapel; at Annapolis only Protestant services are held on the reservation, midshipmen of other religious persuasions attend the churches of the city of Annapolis. These facts indicate that both schools since their earliest beginnings have maintained and enforced a pattern of participation in formal worship. . . .

The prohibition of enactments respecting the establishment of religion does not bar every friendly gesture between church and state. It is not an absolute prohibition against every conceivable situation where the two may work together, any more than the other provisions of the First Amendment—free speech, free press—are absolutes. If abuses occur, such as the use of the instruction hour for sectarian purposes, I have no doubt, in view of the *Ring* case, that Illinois will promptly correct them. If they are of a kind that tend to the establishment of a church or interfere with the free exercise of religion, this Court is open for a review of any erroneous decision. This Court cannot be too cautious in upsetting practices embedded in our society by many years of experience. A state is entitled to have great leeway in its legislation when dealing with the important social problems of its population. A definite violation of legislative limits must be established. The Constitution should not be stretched to forbid national customs in the way courts act to reach arrangements to avoid federal taxation. Devotion to the great principle of religious liberty should not lead us into a rigid interpretation of the constitutional guarantee that conflicts with accepted habits of our people. This is an instance where, for me, the history of past practices is determinative of the meaning of a constitutional clause, not a decorous introduction to the study of its text. The judgment should be affirmed.

6

Zorach v. Clauson

343 U.S. 306 (1952)

Appeal from the Court of Appeals of New York.

MR. JUSTICE DOUGLAS delivered the opinion of the Court.

New York City has a program which permits its public schools to release students during the school day so that they may leave the school buildings and school grounds and go to religious centers for religious instruction or devotional exercises. A student is released on written request of his parents. Those not released stay in the classrooms. The churches make weekly reports to the schools, sending a list of children who have been released from public school but who have not reported for religious instruction.

This "released time" program involves neither religious instruction in public school classrooms nor the expenditure of public funds. All costs, including the application blanks, are paid by the religious organizations. The case is therefore unlike *McCollum* v. *Board of Education,* 333 U.S. 203, which involved a "released time" program from Illinois. In that case the classrooms were turned over to religious instructors. We accordingly held that the program violated the First Amendment which (by reason of the Fourteenth Amendment) prohibits the states from establishing religion or prohibiting its free exercise.

Appellants, who are taxpayers and residents of New York City and whose children attend its public schools, challenge the present law, contending it is in essence not different from the one involved in the *McCollum* case. Their argument, stated elaborately in various ways, reduces itself to this: the weight and influence of the school is put behind a program for religious instruction; public school teachers police it, keeping tab on students who are released; the classroom activities come to a halt while the students who are released for religious instruction are on leave; the school is a crutch on which the churches are leaning for support in their religious training; without the cooperation of the schools this "released time" program, like the one in the *McCollum* case, would be futile and ineffective. The New York Court of Appeals sustained the law against this claim of unconstitutionality. . . .

The briefs and arguments are replete with data bearing on the merits of this type of "released time" program. Views *pro* and *con* are expressed, based on practical experience with these programs and with their implications. We do not stop to summarize these materials nor to burden the opinion with an analysis of them. For they involve considerations not germane to the narrow constitutional issue presented. They largely concern the wisdom of the system, its efficiency from an educational point of view, and the political considerations which have motivated its adoption or rejection in some communities. Those matters are of no concern here, since our problem reduces itself to whether New York by this system has either prohibited the "free exercise" of religion or has made a law "respecting an establishment of religion" within the meaning of the First Amendment.

It takes obtuse reasoning to inject any issue of the "free exercise" of religion into the present case. No one is forced to go to the religious classroom and no religious exercise or instruction is brought to the classrooms of the public schools. A student need not take religious instruction. He is left to his own desires as to the manner or time of his religious devotions, if any.

There is a suggestion that the system involves the use of coercion to get public school students into religious classrooms. There is no evidence in the record before us that supports that conclusion. The present record indeed tells us that the school authorities are neutral in this regard and do no more than release students whose parents so request. If in fact coercion were used, if it were established that any one or more teachers were using their office to persuade or force students to take the religious instruction, a wholly different case would be presented. Hence we put aside that claim of coercion both as respects the "free exercise" of religion and "an establishment of religion" within the meaning of the First Amendment.

Moreover, apart from that claim of coercion, we do not see how New York by this type of "released time" program has made a law respecting an establishment of religion within the meaning of the First Amendment. There is much talk of the separation of Church and State in the history of the Bill of Rights and in the decisions clustering around the First Amendment. . . . There cannot be the slightest doubt that the First Amendment reflects the philosophy that Church and State should be separated. And so far as interference with the "free exercise" of religion and an "establishment" of religion are concerned, the separation must be complete and unequivocal. The First Amendment within the scope of its coverage permits no exception; the prohibition is absolute. The First Amendment, however, does not say that in every and all respects there shall be a separation of Church and State. Rather, it studiously defines the manner, the specific ways, in which there shall be no concert or union or dependency one on the other. That is the common sense of the matter. Otherwise the state and religion would be aliens to each other—hostile, suspicious, and even unfriendly. Churches could not be required to pay even property taxes. Municipalities would not be permitted to render police or fire protection to religious groups. Policemen who helped parishioners into their places of worship would violate the Constitution. Prayers in our legislative halls; the appeals to the Almighty in the messages of the Chief Executive; the proclamations making Thanksgiving Day a holiday; "so help me God" in our courtroom oaths—these and all other references to the Almighty that run through our laws, our public rituals, our ceremonies would be flouting the First Amendment. A fastidious atheist or agnostic could even object to the supplication with which the Court opens each session: "God save the United States and this Honorable Court."

We would have to press the concept of separation of Church and State to these extremes to condemn the present law on constitutional grounds. The nullification of this law would have wide and profound effects. A Catholic student applies to his teacher for permission to leave the school during hours on a Holy Day of Obligation to attend a mass. A Jewish student asks his teacher for permission to be excused for Yom Kippur. A Protestant wants the afternoon off for a family baptismal ceremony. In each case the teacher requires parental consent in writing. In each case the teacher, in order to make sure the student is not a truant, goes further and requires a report from the priest, the rabbi, or the minister. The teacher in other words cooperates in a religious program to the extent of making it possible for her students to participate in it. Whether she does it occasionally for a few students, regularly for one, or pursuant to a systematized program designed to further the religious needs of all the students does not alter the character of the act.

We are a religious people whose institutions presuppose a Supreme Being. We guarantee the freedom to worship as one chooses. We make room for as wide a variety of beliefs and creeds as the spiritual needs of man deem necessary. We sponsor an attitude on the part of government that shows no partiality to any one group and that lets each flourish according to the zeal of its adherents and the appeal of its dogma. When the state encourages religious instruction or cooperates with religious authorities by adjusting the schedule of public events to sectarian needs, it follows the best of our traditions. For it then respects the religious nature of our people and accommodates the public service to their spiritual needs. To hold that it may not would be to find in the Constitution a requirement that the government show a callous indifference to religious groups. That would be preferring those who believe in no religion over those who do believe. Government may not finance religious groups nor undertake religious instruction nor blend secular and sectarian education nor use secular institutions to force one or some religion on any person. But we find no constitutional requirement which makes it necessary for government to be hostile to religion and to throw its weight against efforts to widen the effective scope of religious influence. The government must be neutral when it comes to competition between sects. It may not thrust any sect on any person. It may not make a religious observance compulsory. It may not coerce anyone to attend church, to observe a religious holiday, or to take religious instruction. But it can close its doors or suspend its operations as to those who want to repair to their religious sanctuary for worship or instruction. No more than that is undertaken here.

This program may be unwise and improvident from an educational or a community viewpoint. . . . Our individual preferences, however, are not the constitutional standard. The constitutional standard is the separation of Church and State. The problem, like many problems in constitutional law, is one of degree. . . .

Affirmed.

MR. JUSTICE BLACK, dissenting.

I see no significant difference between the invalid Illinois system and that of New York here sustained. Except for the use of the school buildings in Illinois, there is no difference between the systems which I consider even worthy of mention. In the New York program, as in that of Illinois, the school authorities release some of the children on the condition that they attend the religious classes, get reports on whether they attend, and hold the other children in the school building until the religious hour is over. As we attempted to make categorically clear, the *McCollum* decision would have been the same if the religious classes had not been held in the school buildings.

I am aware that our *McCollum* decision on separation of Church and State has been subjected to a most searching examination throughout the country. Probably few opinions from this Court in recent years have attracted more attention or stirred wider debate. Our insistence on "a wall between Church and State which must be kept high and impregnable" has seemed to some a correct exposition of the philosophy and a true interpretation of the language of the First Amendment to which we should strictly adhere. With equal conviction and sincerity, others have thought the *McCollum* decision fundamentally wrong and have pledged continuous warfare against it. The opinions in the court below and the briefs here reflect these diverse viewpoints. In dissenting today, I mean to do more than give routine approval to our *McCollum* decision. I mean also to reaffirm my faith in the fundamental philosophy expressed in *McCollum* and *Everson* v. *Board of Education,* 330 U.S. 1. . . .

Here the sole question is whether New York can use its compulsory education laws to help religious sects get attendants presumably too unenthusiastic to go unless moved to do so by the pressure of this state machinery. That this is the plan, purpose, design and consequence of the New York program cannot be denied. The state thus makes religious sects beneficiaries of its power to compel children to attend secular schools. Any use of such coercive power by the state to help or hinder some religious sects or to prefer all religious sects over non-believers or vice versa is just what I think the First Amendment forbids. In considering whether a state has entered this forbidden field the question is not whether it has entered too far but whether it has entered at all. New York is manipulating its compulsory education laws to help religious sects get pupils. This is not separation but combination of Church and State.

The Court's validation of the New York system rests in part on its statement that Americans are "a religious people whose institutions presuppose a Supreme Being." This was at least as true when the First Amendment was adopted; and it was just as true when eight Justices of this Court invalidated the released time system in *Mc-*

Collum on the premise that a state can no more "aid all religions" than it can aid one. It was precisely because Eighteenth Century Americans were a religious people divided into many fighting sects that we were given the constitutional mandate to keep Church and State completely separate. Colonial history had already shown that, here as elsewhere zealous sectarians entrusted with governmental power to further their causes would sometimes torture, maim and kill those they branded "heretics," "atheists" or "agnostics." The First Amendment was therefore to insure that no one powerful sect or combination of sects could use political or governmental power to punish dissenters whom they could not convert to their faith. Now as then, it is only by wholly isolating the state from the religious sphere and compelling it to be completely neutral, that the freedom of each and every denomination and of all nonbelievers can be maintained. It is this neutrality the Court abandons today when it treats New York's coercive system as a program which *merely* "encourages religious instruction or cooperates with religious authorities." The abandonment is all the more dangerous to liberty because of the Court's legal exaltation of the orthodox and its derogation of unbelievers.

Under our system of religious freedom, people have gone to their religious sanctuaries not because they feared the law but because they loved their God. The choice of all has been as free as the choice of those who answered the call to worship moved only by the music of the old Sunday morning church bells. The spiritual mind of man has thus been free to believe, disbelieve, or doubt, without repression, great or small, by the heavy hand of government. Statutes authorizing such repression have been stricken. Before today, our judicial opinions have refrained from drawing invidious distinctions between those who believe in no religion and those who do believe. The First Amendment has lost much if the religious follower and the atheist are no longer to be judicially regarded as entitled to equal justice under the law.

State help to religion injects political and party prejudices into a holy field. It too often substitutes force for prayer, hate for love, and persecution for persuasion. Government should not be allowed, under cover of the soft euphemism of "cooperation," to steal into the sacred area of religious choice.

MR. JUSTICE FRANKFURTER, dissenting.

Of course, a State may provide that the classes in its schools shall be dismissed, for any reason, or no reason, on fixed days, or for special occasions. The essence of this case is that the school system did not "close its doors" and did not "suspend its operations." There is all the difference in the world between letting the children out of school and letting some of them out of school into religious classes. If every one is free to make what use he will of time wholly unconnected from schooling required by law—those who wish sectarian instruction devoting it to that purpose, those who have ethical instruction at home, to that, those who study music, to that—then of course there is no conflict with the Fourteenth Amendment.

The pith of the case is that formalized religious instruction is substituted for other school activity which those who do not participate in the released-time program are compelled to attend. The school system is very much in operation during this kind of released time. If its doors are closed, they are closed upon those students who do not attend the religious instruction, in order to keep them within the school. That is the very thing which raises the constitutional issue. It is not met by disregarding it. Failure to discuss this issue does not take it out of the case. . . .

The deeply divisive controversy aroused by the attempts to secure public school pupils for sectarian instruction would promptly end if the advocates of such instruction were content to have the school "close its doors or suspend its operations"—that is, dismiss classes in their entirety, without discrimination—instead of seeking to use the public schools as the instrument for securing attendance at denominational classes. The unwillingness of the promoters of this movement to dispense with such use of the public schools betrays a surprising want of confidence in the inherent power of the various faiths to draw children to outside sectarian classes—an attitude that hardly reflects the faith of the greatest religious spirits.

MR. JUSTICE JACKSON, dissenting.

This released time program is founded upon a use of the State's power of coercion, which, for me, determines its unconstitutionality. . . .

If public education were taking so much of the pupils' time as to injure the public or the students' welfare by encroaching upon their religious opportunity, simply shortening everyone's school day would facilitate voluntary and optional attendance at Church classes. But that suggestion is rejected upon the ground that if they are made free many students will not go to the Church. Hence, they must be deprived of freedom for this period, with Church attendance put to them as one of the two permissible ways of using it.

The greater effectiveness of this system over voluntary attendance after school hours is due to the truant officer who, if the youngster fails to go to the Church school, dogs him back to the public schoolroom. Here schooling is more or less suspended during the "released time" so that nonreligious attendants will not forge ahead of the churchgoing absentees. But it serves as a temporary jail for a pupil who will not go to Church. It takes more subtlety of mind than I possess to deny that this is governmental constraint in support of religion. It is as unconstitutional, in my view, when exerted by indirection as when exercised forthrightly.

As one whose children, as a matter of free choice, have been sent to privately supported Church schools, I may challenge the Court's suggestion that opposition to this plan can only be antireligious, atheistic, or agnostic. My evangelistic brethren confuse an objection to compulsion with an objection to religion. It is possible to hold a faith with enough confidence to believe that what should be rendered to God does not need to be decided and collected by Caesar.

The day that this country ceases to be free for irreligion it will cease to be free for religion—except for the sect that can win political power. The same epithetical jurisprudence used by the Court today to beat down those who oppose pressuring children into some religion can devise as good epithets tomorrow against those who object to pressuring them into a favored religion. And, after all, if we concede to the State power and wisdom to single out "duly constituted religious" bodies as exclusive alternatives for compulsory secular instruction, it would be logical to also uphold the power and wisdom to choose the true faith among those "duly constituted." We start down a rough road when we begin to mix compulsory public education with compulsory godliness. . . .

The wall which the Court was professing to erect between Church and State has become even more warped and twisted than I expected. Today's judgment will be more interesting to students of psychology and of the judicial processes than to students of constitutional law.

Part II

EDUCATION AND RACIAL SEGREGATION

7

Sweatt v. Painter

339 U.S. 629 (1950)

Certiorari to the Supreme Court of Texas.

MR. CHIEF JUSTICE VINSON delivered the opinion of a unanimous Court.

This case and *McLaurin* v. *Oklahoma State Regents,* . . . present differing aspects of this general question: To what extent does the Equal Protection Clause of the Fourteenth Amendment limit the power of a state to distinguish between students of different races in professional and graduate education in a state university? Broader issues have been urged for our consideration, but we adhere to the principle of deciding constitutional questions only in the context of the particular case before the Court. We have frequently reiterated that this Court will decide constitutional questions only when necessary to the disposition of the case at hand, and that such decisions will be drawn as narrowly as possible. . . . Because of this traditional reluctance to extend constitutional interpretations to situations or facts which are not before the Court, much of the excellent research and detailed argument presented in these cases is unnecessary to their disposition.

In the instant case, petitioner filed an application for admission to the University of Texas Law School for the February, 1946 term. His application was rejected solely because he is a Negro. Petitioner thereupon brought this suit for mandamus against the appropriate school officials, respondents here, to compel his admission. At that time, there was no law school in Texas which admitted Negroes.

The State trial court recognized that the action of the State in denying petitioner the opportunity to gain a legal education while granting it to others deprived him of the equal protection of the laws guaranteed by the

Fourteenth Amendment. The court did not grant the relief requested, however, but continued the case for six months to allow the State to supply substantially equal facilities. At the expiration of the six months, in December, 1946, the court denied the writ on the showing that the authorized university officials had adopted an order calling for the opening of a law school for Negroes the following February. While petitioner's appeal was pending, such a school was made available, but petitioner refused to register therein. The Texas Court of Civil Appeals set aside the trial court's judgment and ordered the cause "remanded generally to the trial court for further proceedings without prejudice to the rights of any party to this suit."

On remand, a hearing was held on the issue of the equality of the educational facilities at the newly established school as compared with the University of Texas Law School. Finding that the new school offered petitioner "privileges, advantages, and opportunities for the study of law substantially equivalent to those offered by the State to white students at the University of Texas," the trial court denied mandamus. The Court of Civil Appeals affirmed. . . .

The University of Texas Law School, from which petitioner was excluded, was staffed by a faculty of sixteen full-time and three part-time professors, some of whom are nationally recognized authorities in their field. Its student body numbered 850. The library contained over 65,000 volumes. Among the other facilities available to the students were a law review, moot court facilities, scholarship funds, and Order of the Coif affiliation. The school's alumni occupy the most distinguished positions in the private practice of the law and in the public life of the State. It may properly be considered one of the nation's ranking law schools.

The law school for Negroes which was to have opened in February, 1947, would have had no independent faculty or library. The teaching was to be carried on by four members of the University of Texas Law School faculty, who were to maintain their offices at the University of Texas while teaching at both institutions. Few of the 10,000 volumes ordered for the library had arrived; nor was there any full-time librarian. The school lacked accreditation.

Since the trial of this case, respondents report the opening of a law school at the Texas State University for Negroes. It is apparently on the road to full accreditation. It has a faculty of five full-time professors; a student body of 23; a library of some 16,500 volumes serviced by a full-time staff; a practice court and legal aid association; and one alumnus who has become a member of the Texas Bar.

Whether the University of Texas Law School is compared with the original or the new law school for Negroes, we cannot find substantial equality in the educational opportunities offered white and Negro law students by the State. In terms of number of the faculty, variety of courses and opportunity for specialization, size of the student body, scope of the library, availability of law review and similar activities, the University of Texas Law School is superior. What is more important, the University of Texas Law School possesses to a far greater degree those qualities which are incapable of objective measurement but which make for greatness in a law school. Such qualities, to name but a few, include reputation of the faculty, experience of the administration, position and influence of the alumni, standing in the community, traditions and prestige. It is difficult to believe that one who had a free choice between these law schools would consider the question close.

Moreover, although the law is a highly learned profession, we are well aware that it is an intensely practical one. The law school, the proving ground for legal learning and practice, cannot be effective in isolation from the individuals and institutions with which the law interacts. Few students and no one who has practiced law would choose to study in an academic vacuum, removed from the interplay of ideas and the exchange of views with which the law is concerned. The law school to which Texas is willing to admit petitioner excludes from its student body members of the racial groups which number 85 per cent of the population of the State and include most of the lawyers, witnesses, jurors, judges, and other officials with whom petitioner will inevitably be dealing when he becomes a member of the Texas Bar. With such a substantial and significant segment of society excluded, we cannot conclude that the education offered petitioner is substantially equal to that which he would receive if admitted to the University of Texas Law School.

It may be argued that excluding petitioner from that school is no different from excluding white students from the new law school. This contention overlooks realities. It is unlikely that a member of a group so decisively in the majority, attending a school with rich traditions and prestige which only a history of consistently maintained excellence could command, would claim that the opportunities afforded him for legal education were unequal to those held open to petitioner. That such a claim, if made, would be dishonored by the State, is no answer. "Equal protection of the laws is not achieved through indiscriminate imposition of inequalities." *Shelley* v. *Kraemer,* 334 U.S. 1, 22 (1948).

It is fundamental that these cases concern rights which are personal and present. This Court has stated unanimously that "The State must provide [legal education] for [petitioner] in conformity with the equal protection clause of the Fourteenth Amendment and provide it as soon as it does for applicants of any other group." *Sipuel* v. *Board of Regents,* 332 U.S. 631, 633 (1948). That case "did not present the issue whether a state might not satisfy the equal protection clause of the Fourteenth Amendment by establishing a separate law school for Negroes." *Fisher* v. *Hurst,* 333 U.S. 147, 150 (1948). In *Missouri ex rel. Gaines* v. *Canada,* 305 U.S. 337, 351 (1938), the Court, speaking through Chief Justice Hughes, declared that "petitioner's right was a personal one. It was as an individual that he was entitled to the equal protection of the laws, and the State was bound to furnish him within its borders facilities for legal education substantially equal to those which the State there afforded for persons of the white race, whether or not other Negroes sought the same opportunity." These are the only cases in this Court which present the issue of the constitutional validity of race distinctions in state-supported graduate and professional education.

In accordance with these cases, petitioner may claim his full constitutional right: legal education equivalent to that offered by the State to students of other races. Such education is not available to him in a separate law school as offered by the State. We cannot, therefore, agree with respondents that the doctrine of *Plessy* v. *Ferguson,* 163 U.S. 537 (1896) requires affirmance of the judgment below. Nor need we reach petitioner's contention that *Plessy* v. *Ferguson* should be reexamined in the light of contemporary knowledge respecting the purposes of the Fourteenth Amendment and the effects of racial segregation. . . .

We hold that the Equal Protection Clause of the Fourteenth Amendment requires that petitioner be admitted to the University of Texas Law School. The judgment is reversed and the cause is remanded for proceedings not inconsistent with this opinion.

Reversed.

8

Brown v. Board of Education

347 U.S. 483 (1954)

Appeal from the U.S. District Court for the District of Kansas.

Appeal from the U.S. District Court for the Eastern District of South Carolina.

Appeal from the U.S. District Court for the Eastern District of Virginia.

Certiorari to the Supreme Court of Delaware.

MR. CHIEF JUSTICE WARREN delivered the opinion of a unanimous Court.

These cases come to us from the States of Kansas, South Carolina, Virginia, and Delaware. They are premised on different facts and different local conditions, but a common legal question justifies their consideration together in this consolidated opinion.

In each of the cases, minors of the Negro race, through their legal representatives, seek the aid of the courts in obtaining admission to the public schools of their community on a nonsegregated basis. In each instance, they had been denied admission to schools attended by white children under laws requiring or permitting segregation according to race. This segregation was alleged to deprive the plaintiffs of the equal protection of the laws under the Fourteenth Amendment. In each of the cases other than the Delaware case, a three-judge federal district court denied relief to the plaintiffs on the so-called "separate but equal" doctrine announced by this Court in *Plessy* v. *Ferguson,* 163 U.S. 537. Under that doctrine, equality of treatment is accorded when the races are provided substantially equal facilities, even though these facilities be separate. . . .

The plaintiffs contend that segregated public schools are not "equal" and cannot be made "equal," and that hence they are deprived of the equal protection of the laws. Because of the obvious importance of the question presented, the Court took jurisdiction. Argument was heard in the 1952 Term, and reargument was heard this Term on certain questions propounded by the Court.

Reargument was largely devoted to the circumstances surrounding the adoption of the Fourteenth Amendment in 1868. It covered exhaustively consideration of the Amendment in Congress, ratification by the states, then existing practices in racial segregation, and the views of proponents and opponents of the Amendment. This discussion and our own investigation convince us that, although these sources cast some light, it is not enough to resolve the problem with which we are faced. At best, they are inconclusive. The most avid proponents of the post-War Amendments undoubtedly intended them to remove all legal distinctions among "all persons born or naturalized in the United States." Their opponents, just as certainly, were antagonistic to both the letter and the spirit of the Amendments and wished them to have the most limited effect. What others in Congress and the state legislatures had in mind cannot be determined with any degree of certainty.

An additional reason for the inconclusive nature of the Amendment's history, with respect to segregated schools, is the status of public education at that time. In the South, the movement toward free common schools, supported by general taxation, had not yet taken hold. Education of white children was largely in the hands of private groups. Education of Negroes was almost nonexistent, and practically all of the race were illiterate. In fact, any education of Negroes was forbidden by law in some states. Today, in contrast, many Negroes have achieved outstanding success in the arts and sciences as well as in the business and professional world. It is true that public school education at the time of the Amendment had advanced further in the North, but the effect of the Amendment on Northern States was generally ignored in the congressional debates. Even in the North, the conditions of public education did not approximate those existing today. The curriculum was usually rudimentary; ungraded schools were common in rural areas;

the school term was but three months a year in many states; and compulsory school attendance was virtually unknown. As a consequence, it is not surprising that there should be so little in the history of the Fourteenth Amendment relating to its intended effect on public education.

In the first cases in this Court construing the Fourteenth Amendment, decided shortly after its adoption, the Court interpreted it as proscribing all state-imposed discriminations against the Negro race. The doctrine of "separate but equal" did not make its appearance in this Court until 1896 in the case of *Plessy* v. *Ferguson,* . . . involving not education but transportation. American courts have since labored with the doctrine for over half a century. In this Court, there have been six cases involving the "separate but equal" doctrine in the field of public education. In *Cumming* v. *County Board of Education,* 175 U.S. 528, and *Gong Lum* v. *Rice,* 275 U.S. 78, the validity of the doctrine itself was not challenged. In more recent cases, all on the graduate school level, inequality was found in that specific benefits enjoyed by white students were denied to Negro students of the same educational qualifications. *Missouri ex rel. Gaines* v. *Canada,* 305 U.S. 337; *Sipuel* v. *Oklahoma,* 332 U.S. 631; *Sweatt* v. *Painter,* 339 U.S. 629; *McLaurin* v. *Oklahoma State Regents,* 339 U.S. 637. In none of these cases was it necessary to reexamine the doctrine to grant relief to the Negro plaintiff. And in *Sweatt* v. *Painter,* . . . the Court expressly reserved decision on the question whether *Plessy* v. *Ferguson* should be held inapplicable to public education.

In the instant cases, that question is directly presented. Here, unlike *Sweatt* v. *Painter,* there are findings below that the Negro and white schools involved have been equalized, or are being equalized, with respect to buildings, curricula, qualifications and salaries of teachers, and other "tangible" factors. Our decision, therefore, cannot turn on merely a comparison of these tangible factors in the Negro and white schools involved in each of the cases. We must look instead to the effect of segregation itself on public education.

In approaching this problem, we cannot turn the clock back to 1868 when the Amendment was adopted, or even to 1896 when *Plessy* v. *Ferguson* was written. We must consider public education in the light of its full development and its present place in American life throughout the Nation. Only in this way can it be determined if segregation in public schools deprives these plaintiffs of the equal protection of the laws.

Today, education is perhaps the most important function of state and local governments. Compulsory school attendance laws and the great expenditures for education both demonstrate our recognition of the importance of education to our democratic society. It is required in the performance of our most basic public responsibilities, even service in the armed forces. It is the very foundation of good citizenship. Today it is a principal instrument in awakening the child to cultural values, in preparing him for later professional training, and in helping him to adjust normally to his environment. In these days, it is doubtful that any child may reasonably be expected to succeed in life if he is denied the opportunity of an education. Such an opportunity, where the state has undertaken to provide it, is a right which must be made available to all on equal terms.

We come then to the question presented: Does segregation of children in public schools solely on the basis of race, even though the physical facilities and other "tangible" factors may be equal, deprive the children of the minority group of equal educational opportunities? We believe that it does.

In *Sweatt* v. *Painter,* in finding that a segregated law school for Negroes could not provide them equal educational opportunities, this Court relied in large part on "those qualities which are incapable of objective measurement but which make for greatness in a law school." In *McLaurin* v. *Oklahoma State Regents,* the Court, in requiring that a Negro admitted to a white graduate school be treated like all other students, again resorted to intangible considerations: "his ability to study, to engage in discussions and exchange views with other students, and, in general, to learn his profession." Such considerations apply with added force to children in grade and high schools. To separate them from others of similar age and qualifications solely because of their race generates a feeling of inferiority as to their status in the community that may affect their hearts and minds in a way unlikely ever to be undone. The effect of this separation on their educational opportunities was well stated by a finding in the Kansas case by a court which nevertheless felt compelled to rule against the Negro plaintiffs:

> Segregation of white and colored children in public schools has a detrimental effect upon the colored children. The impact is greater when it has the sanction of the law; for the policy of separating the races is usually interpreted as denoting the inferiority of the negro group. A sense of inferiority affects the motivation of a child to learn. Segregation with the sanction of law, therefore, has a tendency to [retard] the educational and mental development of negro children and to deprive them of some of the benefits they would receive in a racial[ly] integrated school system.

Whatever may have been the extent of psychological knowledge at the time of *Plessy* v. *Ferguson,* this finding is amply supported by modern authority.[11] Any language in *Plessy* v. *Ferguson* contrary to this finding is rejected.

---

[11] K. B. Clark, *Effect of Prejudice and Discrimination on Personality Development* (Midcentury White House Conference on Children and Youth, 1950); Witmer and Kotinsky, *Personality in the Making* (1952), Chap. 6; Deutscher and Chein, "The Psychological Effects of Enforced Segregation: A Survey of Social Science Opinion," 26 *J. Psychol.* 259 (1948); Chein, "What Are the Psychological Effects of Segregation under Conditions of Equal Facilities?" 3 *Int. J. Opinion and Attitude Res.* 229 (1949); Brameld, *Educational Costs,* in *Discrimination and National Welfare* (MacIver, ed., 1949), 44-48; Frazier, *The Negro in the United States* (1949), 674-681. And see generally Myrdal, *An American Dilemma* (1944).

We conclude that in the field of public education the doctrine of "separate but equal" has no place. Separate educational facilities are inherently unequal. Therefore, we hold that the plaintiffs and others similarly situated for whom the actions have been brought are, by reason of the segregation complained of, deprived of the equal protection of the laws guaranteed by the Fourteenth Amendment. This disposition makes unnecessary any discussion whether such segregation also violates the Due Process Clause of the Fourteenth Amendment.

Because these are class actions, because of the wide applicability of this decision, and because of the great variety of local conditions, the formulation of decrees in these cases presents problems of considerable complexity. On reargument, the consideration of appropriate relief was necessarily subordinated to the primary question—the constitutionality of segregation in public education. We have now announced that such segregation is a denial of the equal protection of the laws. In order that we may have the full assistance of the parties in formulating decrees, the cases will be restored to the docket, and the parties are requested to present further argument. . . . The Attorney General of the United States is again invited to participate. The Attorneys General of the states requiring or permitting segregation in public education will also be permitted to appear as *amici curiae* upon request to do so. . . .

It is so ordered.

9

Brown v. Board of Education

349 U.S. 294 (1955)

Appeal from the United States District Court for the District of Kansas, the United States District Court for the Eastern District of South Carolina, and from the United States District Court for the Eastern District of Virginia.

Certiorari to the United States Court of Appeals for the District of Columbia Circuit and to the Supreme Court of Delaware.

MR. CHIEF JUSTICE WARREN delivered the opinion of a unanimous Court.

These cases were decided on May 17, 1954. The opinions of that date, declaring the fundamental principle that racial discrimination in public education is unconstitutional, are incorporated herein by reference. All provisions of federal, state, or local law requiring or permitting such discrimination must yield to this principle. There remains for consideration the manner in which relief is to be accorded.

Because these cases arose under different local conditions and their disposition will involve a variety of local problems, we requested further argument on the question of relief. In view of the nationwide importance of the decision, we invited the Attorney General of the United States and the Attorneys General of all states requiring or permitting racial discrimination in public education to present their views on that question. The parties, the United States, and the States of Florida, North Carolina, Arkansas, Oklahoma, Maryland, and Texas filed briefs and participated in the oral argument.

These presentations were informative and helpful to the Court in its consideration of the complexities arising from the transition to a system of public education freed of racial discrimination. The presentations also demonstrated that substantial steps to eliminate racial discrimination in public schools have already been taken. . . .

Full implementation of these constitutional principles may require solution of varied local school problems. School authorities have the primary responsibility for elucidating, assessing, and solving these problems; courts will have to consider whether the action of school authorities constitutes good faith implementation of the governing constitutional principles. Because of their proximity to local conditions and the possible need for further hearings, the courts which originally heard these cases can best perform this judicial appraisal. Accordingly, we believe it appropriate to remand the cases to those courts.

In fashioning and effectuating the decrees, the courts will be guided by equitable principles. Traditionally, equity has been characterized by a practical flexibility in shaping its remedies and by a facility for adjusting and reconciling public and private needs. These cases call for the exercise of these traditional attributes of equity power. At stake is the personal interest of the plaintiffs in admission to public schools as soon as practicable on a nondiscriminatory basis. To effectuate this interest may call for elimination of a variety of obstacles in making the transition to school systems operated in accordance with the constitutional principles set forth in our May 17, 1954, decision. Courts of equity may properly take into account the public interest in the elimination of such obstacles in a systematic and effective manner. But it should go without saying that the vitality of these constitutional principles cannot be allowed to yield simply because of disagreement with them.

While giving weight to these public and private considerations, the courts will require that the defendants make a prompt and reasonable start toward full compliance with our May 17, 1954, ruling. Once such a start has been made, the courts may find that additional time is necessary to carry out the ruling in an effective manner. The burden rests upon the defendants to establish that such time is necessary in the public interest and is consistent with good faith compliance at the earliest practicable date. To that end, the courts may consider problems related to administration, arising from the physical condition of the school plant, the school transportation system, personnel, revision of school districts and attendance areas into compact units to achieve a system of determining admission to the public schools on a nonracial basis, and revision of local laws and regulations which may be necessary in solving the foregoing problems. They will also consider the adequacy of any plans the defendants may propose to meet these problems and to effectuate a transition to a racially nondiscriminatory school system. During this period of transition, the courts will retain jurisdiction of these cases. . . .

The judgments below, except that in the Delaware case, are accordingly reversed and the cases are remanded to the District Courts to take such proceedings and enter such orders and decrees consistent with this opinion as are necessary and proper to admit to public schools on a racially nondiscriminatory basis with all deliberate speed the parties to these cases. The judgment in the Delaware case—ordering the immediate admission of the plaintiffs to schools previously attended only by white children—is affirmed on the basis of the principles stated in our May 17, 1954, opinion, but the case is remanded to the Supreme Court of Delaware for such further proceedings as that Court may deem necessary in light of this opinion.

It is so ordered.

10

Cooper v. Aaron

358 U.S. 1 (1958)

Certiorari to the United States Court of Appeals for the Eighth Circuit.

Opinion of the Court by the CHIEF JUSTICE, MR. JUSTICE BLACK, MR. JUSTICE FRANKFURTER, MR. JUSTICE DOUGLAS, MR. JUSTICE BURTON, MR. JUSTICE CLARK, MR. JUSTICE HARLAN, MR. JUSTICE BRENNAN, and MR. JUSTICE WHITTAKER.

As this case reaches us it raises questions of the highest importance to the maintenance of our federal system of government. It necessarily involves a claim by the Governor and Legislature of a State that there is no duty on state officials to obey federal court orders resting on this Court's considered interpretation of the United States Constitution. Specifically it involves actions by the Governor and Legislature of Arkansas upon the premise that they are not bound by our holding in *Brown* v. *Board of Education,* 347 U.S. 483. That holding was that the Fourteenth Amendment forbids States to use their governmental powers to bar children on racial grounds from attending schools where there is state participation through any arrangement, management, funds or property. We are urged to uphold a suspension of the Little Rock School Board's plan to do away with segregated public schools in Little Rock until state laws and efforts to upset and nullify our holding in *Brown* v. *Board of Education* have been further challenged and tested in the courts. We reject these contentions.

The case was argued before us on September 11, 1958. On the following day we unanimously affirmed the judgment of the Court of Appeals for the Eighth Circuit, which had reversed a judgment of the District Court for the Eastern District of Arkansas. The District Court had granted the application of the petitioners, the Little Rock School Board and School Superintendent, to suspend for two and one-half years the operation of the School Board's court-approved desegregation program. In order that the School Board might know, without doubt, its duty in this regard before the opening of school, which had been set for the following Monday, September 15, 1958, we immediately issued the judgment, reserving the expression of our supporting views to a later date. This opinion of all the members of the Court embodies those views.

The following are the facts and circumstances so far as necessary to show how the legal questions are presented.

On May 20, 1954, three days after the first *Brown* opinion, the Little Rock District School Board adopted, and on May 23, 1954, made public, a statement of policy entitled "Supreme Court Decision—Segregation in Public Schools." In this statement the Board recognized that "It is our responsibility to comply with Federal Constitutional Requirements and we intend to do so when the Supreme Court of the United States outlines the method to be followed."

Thereafter the Board undertook studies of the administrative problems confronting the transition to a desegregated public school system at Little Rock. It instructed the Superintendent of Schools to prepare a plan for desegregation, and approved such a plan on May 24, 1955, seven days before the second *Brown* opinion. The plan provided for desegregation at the senior high school level (grades 10 through 12) as the first stage. Desegregation at the junior high and elementary levels was to follow. It was contemplated that desegregation at the high school level would commence in the fall of 1957, and the expectation was that complete desegregation of the school system would be accomplished by 1963. Following the adoption of this plan, the Superintendent of Schools discussed it with a large number of citizen groups in the city. As a result of these discussions, the Board reached the conclusion that "a large majority of the residents" of Little Rock were of "the belief . . . that the Plan, although objectionable in principle," from the point of view of those supporting segregated schools, "was still the best for the interests of all pupils in the District."

Upon challenge by a group of Negro plaintiffs desiring more rapid completion of the desegregation process, the District Court upheld the School Board's plan, *Aaron* v. *Cooper,* 143 F. Supp. 855. The Court of Appeals affirmed. 243 F2d 361. Review of that judgment was not sought here.

While the School Board was thus going forward with its preparation for desegregating the Little Rock school system, other state authorities, in contrast, were actively pursuing a program designed to perpetuate in Arkansas the system of racial segregation which this Court had held violated the Fourteenth Amendment. First came, in November 1956, an amendment to the State Constitution flatly commanding the Arkansas General Assembly to oppose "in every Constitutional manner the Unconstitutional desegregation decisions of May 17, 1954 and May 31, 1955 of the United States Supreme Court," and, through the initiative, a pupil assignment law. Pursuant to this state constitutional command, a law relieving school children from compulsory attendance at racially mixed schools and a law establishing a State Sovereignty Commission were enacted by the General Assembly in February 1957.

The School Board and the Superintendent of Schools nevertheless continued with preparations to carry out the first stage of the desegregation program. Nine Negro children were scheduled for admission in September 1957 to Central High School, which has more than two thousand students. Various administrative measures, designed to assure the smooth transition of this first stage of desegregation, were undertaken.

On September 2, 1957, the day before these Negro students were to enter Central High, the school authorities were met with drastic opposing action on the part of the Governor of Arkansas who dispatched units of the

Arkansas National Guard to the Central High School grounds, and placed the school "off limits" to colored students. As found by the District Court in subsequent proceedings, the Governor's action had not been requested by the school authorities, and was entirely unheralded.

The next day, September 3, 1957, the Board petitioned the District Court for instructions, and the court, after a hearing, found that the Board's request of the Negro students to stay away from the high school had been made because of the stationing of the military guards by the state authorities. The court determined that this was not a reason for departing from the approved plan, and ordered the School Board and Superintendent to proceed with it.

On the morning of the next day, September 4, 1957, the Negro children attempted to enter the high school but, as the District Court later found, units of the Arkansas National Guard "acting pursuant to the Governor's order, stood shoulder to shoulder at the school grounds and thereby forcibly prevented the nine Negro students . . . from entering," as they continued to do every school day during the following three weeks.

That same day, September 4, 1957, the United States Attorney for the Eastern District of Arkansas was requested by the District Court to begin an immediate investigation in order to fix responsibility for the interference with the orderly implementation of the District Court's direction to carry out the desegregation program. Three days later, September 7, the District Court denied a petition of the School Board and the Superintendent of Schools for an order temporarily suspending continuance of the program.

Upon completion of the United States Attorney's investigation, he and the Attorney General of the United States, at the District Court's request, entered the proceedings and filed a petition on behalf of the United States, as *amicus curiae,* to enjoin the Governor of Arkansas and officers of the Arkansas National Guard from further attempts to prevent obedience to the court's order. After hearings on the petition, the District Court found that the School Board's plan had been obstructed by the Governor through the use of National Guard troops, and granted a preliminary injunction on September 20, 1957, enjoining the Governor and the officers of the Guard from preventing the attendance of Negro children at Central High School, and from otherwise obstructing or interfering with the orders of the court in connection with the plan. . . . The National Guard was then withdrawn from the school.

The next school day was Monday, September 23, 1957. The Negro children entered the high school that morning under the protection of the Little Rock Police Department and members of the Arkansas State Police. But the officers caused the children to be removed from the school during the morning because they had difficulty controlling a large and demonstrating crowd which had gathered at the high school. . . . On September 25, however, the President of the United States dispatched federal troops to Central High School and admission of the Negro students to the school was thereby effected. Regular army troops continued at the high school until November 27, 1957. They were then replaced by federalized National Guardsmen who remained throughout the balance of the school year. Eight of the Negro students remained in attendance at the school throughout the school year.

We come now to the aspect of the proceedings presently before us. On February 20, 1958, the School Board and the Superintendent of Schools filed a petition n the District Court seeking a postponement of their program for desegregation. Their position in essence was that because of extreme public hostility, which they tated had been engendered largely by the official attiudes and actions of the Governor and the Legislature, he maintenance of a sound educational program at Central High School, with the Negro students in attendance, would be impossible. The Board therefore proposed that the Negro students already admitted to the chool be withdrawn and sent to segregated schools, and that all further steps to carry out the Board's desegregation program be postponed for a period later suggested by the Board to be two and one-half years.

After a hearing the District Court granted the relief requested by the Board. . . .

In affirming the judgment of the Court of Appeals which reversed the District Court we have accepted without reservation the position of the School Board, the Superintendent of Schools, and their counsel that they displayed entire good faith in the conduct of these proceedings and in dealing with the unfortunate and distressing sequence of events which has been outlined. We likewise have accepted the findings of the District Court as to the conditions at Central High School during the 1957-1958 school year, and also the findings that the educational progress of all the students, white and colored, of that school has suffered and will continue to suffer if the conditions which prevailed last year are permitted to continue.

The significance of these findings, however, is to be considered in light of the fact, indisputably revealed by the record before us, that the conditions they depict are directly traceable to the actions of legislators and executive officials of the State of Arkansas, taken in their official capacities, which reflect their own determination to resist this Court's decision in the *Brown* case and which have brought about violent resistance to that decision in Arkansas. In its petition for certiorari filed in this Court, the School Board itself describes the situation in this language: "The legislative, executive, and judicial departments of the state government opposed the desegregation of Little Rock schools by enacting laws, calling out troops, making statements villifying [*sic*] federal law and federal courts, and failing to utilize state law enforcement agencies and judicial processes to maintain public peace."

One may well sympathize with the position of the Board in the face of the frustrating conditions which have confronted it, but, regardless of the Board's good faith, the actions of the other state agencies responsible for those conditions compel us to reject the Board's legal position. Had Central High School been under the direct management of the State itself, it could hardly be suggested that those immediately in charge of the school should be heard to assert their own good faith as a legal excuse for delay in implementing the constitutional rights of these respondents, when vindication of those rights was rendered difficult or impossible by the actions of other state officials. The situation here is in no different posture because the members of the School Board and the Superintendent of Schools are local officials; from the point of view of the Fourteenth Amendment, they stand in this litigation as the agents of the State.

The constitutional rights of respondents are not to be sacrificed or yielded to the violence and disorder which have followed upon the actions of the Governor and Legislature. As this Court said some forty-one years ago in a unanimous opinion in a case involving another aspect of racial segregation: "It is urged that this proposed segregation will promote the public peace by preventing race conflicts. Desirable as this is, and important as is the preservation of the public peace, this aim cannot be accomplished by laws or ordinances which deny rights created or protected by the Federal Constitution." *Buchanan* v. *Warley,* 245 U.S. 60, 81. Thus law and order are not here to be preserved by depriving the Negro children of their constitutional rights. The record before us clearly establishes that the growth of the Board's difficulties to a magnitude beyond its unaided power to control is the product of state action. Those difficulties, as counsel for the Board forthrightly conceded on the oral argument in this Court, can also be brought under control by state action.

The controlling legal principles are plain. The command of the Fourteenth Amendment is that no "State" shall deny to any person within its jurisdiction the equal protection of the laws. "A State acts by its legislative, its executive, or its judicial authorities. It can act in no other way. The constitutional provision, therefore, must mean that no agency of the State, or of the officers or agents by whom its powers are exerted, shall deny to any person within its jurisdiction the equal protection of the laws. Whoever, by virtue of public position under a State government, . . . denies or takes away the equal protection of the laws, violates the constitutional inhibition; and as he acts in the name and for the State, and is clothed with the State's power, his act is that of the State. This must be so, or the constitutional prohibition has no meaning." *Ex parte Virginia,* 100 U.S. 339, 347. Thus the prohibitions of the Fourteenth Amendment extend to all action of the State denying equal protection of the laws; whatever the agency of the State taking the action, . . . or whatever the guise in which it is taken. . . .

In short, the constitutional rights of children not to be discriminated against in school admission on grounds of race or color declared by this Court in the *Brown* case can neither be nullified openly and directly by state legislators or state executive or judicial officers, nor nullified indirectly by them through evasive schemes for segregation whether attempted "ingeniously or ingenuously." . . .

What has been said, in the light of the facts developed, is enough to dispose of the case. However, we should answer the premise of the actions of the Governor and Legislature that they are not bound by our holding in the *Brown* case. It is necessary only to recall some basic constitutional propositions which are settled doctrine.

Article VI of the Constitution makes the Constitution the "supreme Law of the Land." In 1803, Chief Justice Marshall, speaking for a unanimous Court, referring to the Constitution as "the fundamental and paramount law of the nation," declared in the notable case of *Marbury* v. *Madison,* 1 Cranch 137, 177, that "It is emphatically the province and duty of the judicial department to say what the law is." This decision declared the basic principle that the federal judiciary is supreme in the exposition of the law of the Constitution, and that principle has ever since been respected by this Court and the Country as a permanent and indispensable feature of our constitutional system. It follows that the interpretation of the Fourteenth Amendment enunciated by this Court in the *Brown* case is the supreme law of the land, and Art. VI of the Constitution makes it of binding effect on the States "any Thing in the Constitution or Laws of any State to the Contrary notwithstanding." Every state legislator and executive and judicial officer is solemnly committed by oath taken pursuant to Art. VI, c1, "to support this Constitution." Chief Justice Taney, speaking for a unanimous Court in 1859, said that this requirement reflected the framers' "anxiety to preserve it [the Constitution] in full force, in all its powers, and to guard against resistance to or evasion of its authority, on the part of a State. . . ." *Ableman* v. *Booth,* 21 How. 506, 524.

No state legislator or executive or judicial officer can war against the Constitution without violating his undertaking to support it. Chief Justice Marshall spoke for a unanimous Court in saying that: "If the legislatures of the several states may, at will, annul the judgments of the courts of the United States, and destroy the rights acquired under those judgments, the Constitution itself becomes a solemn mockery. . . ." *United States* v. *Peters,* 5 Cranch 115, 136. A Governor who asserts a power to nullify a federal court order is similarly restrained. If he had such power, said Chief Justice Hughes, in 1932, also for a unanimous Court, "it is manifest that the fiat of a state Governor, and not the Constitution of the United States, would be the supreme law of the land; that the restrictions of the Federal Constitution upon the exercise of state power would be but impotent phrases." *Sterling* v. *Constantin,* 287 U.S. 378, 397-398.

It is, of course, quite true that the responsibility for public education is primarily the concern of the States, but it is equally true that such responsibilities, like all other state activity, must be exercised consistently with federal constitutional requirements as they apply to state action. The Constitution created a government dedicated to equal justice under law. The Fourteenth

Amendment embodied and emphasized that ideal. State support of segregated schools through any arrangement, management, funds, or property cannot be squared with the Amendment's command that no State shall deny to any person within its jurisdiction the equal protection of the laws. The right of a student not to be segregated on racial grounds in schools so maintained is indeed so fundamental and pervasive that it is embraced in the concept of due process of law. *Bolling* v. *Sharpe,* 347 U.S. 497. The basic decision in *Brown* was unanimously reached by this Court only after the case had been briefed and twice argued and the issues had been given the most serious consideration. Since the first *Brown* opinion three new Justices have come to the Court. They are at one with the Justices still on the Court who participated in that basic decision as to its correctness, and that decision is now unanimously reaffirmed. The principles announced in that decision and the obedience of the States to them, according to the command of the Constitution, are indispensable for the protection of the freedoms guaranteed by our fundamental charter for all of us. Our constitutional ideal of equal justice under law is thus made a living truth.

Part III
ACADEMIC FREEDOM

11

Adler v. Board of Education of New York

342 U.S. 485 (1952)

Under §12-a of the Civil Service Law of New York any member of an organization advocating the overthrow of government by force, violence or any unlawful means is ineligible for employment in any public school. To implement this law the legislature adopted the Feinberg Law in 1949. The preamble of this law made elaborate findings that members of subversive groups, particularly of the Communist Party and its affiliated organizations, have been infiltrating into public school employment, to the grave detriment of education. It then provided that the Board of Regents, which has charge of the public school system of the state, shall, after full notice and hearing, make a listing of organizations which it finds advocate, advise, teach or embrace the doctrine that the government should be overthrown by force, violence, or any other unlawful means. The statute then authorized the Board of Regents to provide, by rule, that membership in any listed organization, after notice and hearing, "shall constitute prima facie evidence for disqualification for appointment to or retention in any office or position in the school system." The appellant in this case brought an action for a declaratory judgment asking the state courts to hold the Feinberg Law unconstitutional.

Appeal from the Court of Appeals of New York.

MR. JUSTICE MINTON delivered the opinion of the Court.

It is first argued that the Feinberg Law and the rules promulgated thereunder constitute an abridgment of the freedom of speech and assembly of persons employed or seeking employment in the public schools of the State of New York.

It is clear that such persons have the right under our law to assemble, speak, think and believe as they will. . . . It is equally clear that they have no right to work for the State in the school system on their own terms. . . . They may work for the school system upon the reasonable terms laid down by the proper authorities of New York. If they do not choose to work on such terms, they are at liberty to retain their beliefs and associations and go elsewhere. Has the State thus deprived them of any right to free speech or assembly? We think not. Such persons are or may be denied, under the statutes in question, the privilege of working for the school system of the State of New York because, first, of their advocacy of the overthrow of the government by force or violence, or, secondly, by unexplained membership in an organization found by the school authorities, after notice and hearing, to teach and advocate the overthrow of the government by force or violence, and known by such persons to have such purpose.

The constitutionality of the first proposition is not questioned here. . . .

As to the second, it is rather subtly suggested that we should not follow our recent decision in *Garner* v. *Los Angeles Board,* 341 U.S. 716. We there said:

> We think that a municipal employer is not disabled because it is an agency of the State from inquiring of its employees as to matters that may prove relevant to their fitness and suitability for the public service. Past conduct may well relate to present fitness; past loyalty may have a reasonable relationship to present and future trust. Both are commonly inquired into in determining fitness for both high and low positions in private industry and are not less relevant in public employment. . . .

We adhere to that case. A teacher works in a sensitive area in a schoolroom. There he shapes the attitude of young minds toward the society in which they live. In this, the state has a vital concern. It must preserve the integrity of the schools. That the school authorities have the right and the duty to screen the officials, teachers, and employees as to their fitness to maintain the integrity of the schools as a part of ordered society, cannot be doubted. One's associates, past and present, as well as one's conduct, may properly be considered in determining fitness and loyalty. From time immemorial, one's reputation has been determined in part by the company he keeps. In the employment of officials and teachers of the school system, the state may very properly inquire into the company they keep, and we know of no rule, constitutional or otherwise, that prevents the state, when determining the fitness and loyalty of such persons, from considering the organizations and persons with whom they associate.

If, under the procedure set up in the New York law, a person is found to be unfit and is disqualified from employment in the public school system because of membership in a listed organization, he is not thereby denied the right of free speech and assembly. His freedom of choice between membership in the organization and employment in the school system might be limited, but not his freedom of speech or assembly, except in the remote sense that limitation is inherent in every choice. Certainly such limitation is not one the state may not make in the exercise of its police power to protect the schools from pollution and thereby to defend its own existence.

It is next argued by appellants that the provision in §3022 directing the Board of Regents to provide in rules and regulations that membership in any organization listed by the Board after notice and hearing, with provision for review in accordance with the statute, shall constitute prima facie evidence of disqualification, denies due process, because the fact found bears no relation to the fact presumed. In other words, from the fact found that the organization was one that advocated the overthrow of government by unlawful means and that the person employed or to be employed was a member of the organization and knew of its purpose, to presume that such a member is disqualified for employment is so unreasonable as to be a denial of due process of law. We do not agree. . . .

Membership in a listed organization found to be within the statute and known by the member to be within the statute is a legislative finding that the member by his membership supports the thing the organization stands for, namely, the overthrow of government by unlawful means. We cannot say that such a finding is contrary to fact or that "generality of experience" points to a different conclusion. Disqualification follows therefore as a reasonable presumption from such membership and support. Nor is there here a problem of procedural due process. The presumption is not conclusive but arises only in a hearing where the person against whom it may arise has full opportunity to rebut it. . . .

Where, as here, the relation between the fact found and the presumption is clear and direct and is not conclusive, the requirements of due process are satisfied. . . .

It is also suggested that the use of the word "subversive" is vague and indefinite. But the word is first used in §1 of the Feinberg Law, which is the preamble to the Act, and not in a definitive part thereof. When used in subdivision 2 of §3022, the word has a very definite meaning, namely, an organization that teaches and advocates the overthrow of government by force or violence.

We find no constitutional infirmity in §12-a of the Civil Service Law of New York or in the Feinberg Law which implemented it, and the judgment is

Affirmed.

MR. JUSTICE BLACK, dissenting.

This is another of those rapidly multiplying legislative enactments which make it dangerous—this time for school teachers—to think or say anything except what a transient majority happen to approve at the moment. Basically these laws rest on the belief that government should supervise and limit the flow of ideas into the minds of men. The tendency of such governmental policy is to mould people into a common intellectual pattern.

Quite a different governmental policy rests on the belief that government should leave the mind and spirit of man absolutely free. Such a governmental policy encourages varied intellectual outlooks in the belief that the best views will prevail. This policy of freedom is in my judgment embodied in the First Amendment and made applicable to the states by the Fourteenth. Because of this policy public officials cannot be constitutionally vested with powers to select the ideas people can think about, censor the public views they can express, or choose the persons or groups people can associate with. Public officials with such powers are not public servants; they are public masters.

I dissent from the Court's judgment sustaining this law which effectively penalizes school teachers for their thoughts and their associates.

MR. JUSTICE FRANKFURTER, dissenting.

We are asked to pass on a scheme to counteract what are currently called "subversive" influences in the public school system of New York. The scheme is formulated partly in statutes and partly in administrative regulations, but all of it is still an unfinished blueprint. We are asked to adjudicate claims against its constitutionality before the scheme has been put into operation, before the limits that it imposes upon free inquiry and association, the scope of scrutiny that it sanctions, and the procedural safeguards that will be found to be implied for its enforcement have been authoritatively defined. I think we should adhere to the teaching of this Court's history to avoid constitutional adjudications on merely abstract or speculative issues and to base them on the concreteness afforded by an actual, present, defined controversy, appropriate for judicial judgment, between adversaries immediately affected by it. In accordance with the settled limits upon our jurisdiction I would dismiss this appeal.

MR. JUSTICE DOUGLAS, with whom MR. JUSTICE BLACK concurs, dissenting.

I have not been able to accept the recent doctrine that

a citizen who enters the public service can be forced to sacrifice his civil rights. I cannot for example find in our constitutional scheme the power of a state to place its employees in the category of second-class citizens by denying them freedom of thought and expression. The Constitution guarantees freedom of thought and expression to everyone in our society. All are entitled to it; and none needs it more than the teacher.

The public school is in most respects the cradle of our democracy. The increasing role of the public school is seized upon by proponents of the type of legislation represented by New York's Feinberg law as proof of the importance and need for keeping the school free of "subversive influences." But that is to misconceive the effect of this type of legislation. Indeed the impact of this kind of censorship on the public school system illustrates the high purpose of the First Amendment in freeing speech and thought from censorship.

The present law proceeds on a principle repugnant to our society—guilt by association. A teacher is disqualified because of her membership in an organization found to be "subversive." The finding as to the "subversive" character of the organization is made in a proceeding to which the teacher is not a party and in which it is not clear that she may even be heard. To be sure, she may have a hearing when charges of disloyalty are leveled against her. But in that hearing the finding as to the "subversive" character of the organization apparently may not be reopened in order to allow her to show the truth of the matter. The irrebuttable charge that the organization is "subversive" therefore hangs on as an ominous cloud over her own hearing. The mere fact of membership in the organization raises a prima facie case of her own guilt. She may, it is said, show her innocence. But innocence in this case turns on knowledge; and when the witch hunt is on, one who must rely on ignorance leans on a feeble reed.

The very threat of such a procedure is certain to raise havoc with academic freedom. Youthful indiscretions, mistaken causes, misguided enthusiasms—all long forgotten—become the ghosts of a harrowing present. Any organization committed to a liberal cause, any group organized to revolt against an hysterical trend, any committee launched to sponsor an unpopular program becomes suspect. These are the organizations into which Communists often infiltrate. Their presence infects the whole, even though the project was not conceived in sin. A teacher caught in that mesh is almost certain to stand condemned. Fearing condemnation, she will tend to shrink from any association that stirs controversy. In that manner freedom of expression will be stifled.

But that is only part of it. Once a teacher's connection with a listed organization is shown, her views become subject to scrutiny to determine whether her membership in the organization is innocent or, if she was formerly a member, whether she has *bona fide* abandoned her membership.

The law inevitably turns the school system into a spying project. Regular loyalty reports on the teachers must be made out. The principals become detectives; the students, the parents, the community become informers. Ears are cocked for telltale signs of disloyalty. The prejudices of the community come into play in searching out the disloyal. This is not the usual type of supervision which checks a teacher's competency; it is a system which searches for hidden meanings in a teacher's utterances.

What was the significance of the reference of the art teacher to socialism? Why was the history teacher so openly hostile to Franco Spain? Who heard overtones of revolution in the English teacher's discussion of *The Grapes of Wrath*? What was behind the praise of Soviet progress in metallurgy in the chemistry class? Was it not "subversive" for the teacher to cast doubt on the wisdom of the venture in Korea?

What happens under this law is typical of what happens in a police state. Teachers are under constant surveillance; their pasts are combed for signs of disloyalty; their utterances are watched for clues to dangerous thoughts. A pall is cast over the classrooms. There can be no real academic freedom in that environment. Where suspicion fills the air and holds scholars in line for fear of their jobs, there can be no exercise of the free intellect. Supineness and dogmatism take the place of inquiry. A "party line"—as dangerous as the "party line" of the Communists—lays hold. It is the "party line" of the orthodox view, of the conventional thought, of the accepted approach. A problem can no longer be pursued with impunity to its edges. Fear stalks the classroom. The teacher is no longer a stimulant to adventurous thinking; she becomes instead a pipeline for safe and sound information. A deadening dogma takes the place of free inquiry. Instruction tends to become sterile; pursuit of knowledge is discouraged; discussion often leaves off where it should begin.

This, I think, is what happens when a censor looks over a teacher's shoulder. This system of spying and surveillance with its accompanying reports and trials cannot go hand in hand with academic freedom. It produces standardized thought, not the pursuit of truth. Yet it was the pursuit of truth which the First Amendment was designed to protect. A system which directly or inevitably has that effect is alien to our system and should be struck down. Its survival is a real threat to our way of life. We need be bold and adventuresome in our thinking to survive. A school system producing students trained as robots threatens to rob a generation of the versatility that has been perhaps our greatest distinction. The Framers knew the danger of dogmatism; they also knew the strength that comes when the mind is free, when ideas may be pursued wherever they lead. We forget these teachings of the First Amendment when we sustain this law.

Of course the school systems of the country need not become cells for Communist activities; and the classrooms need not become forums for propagandizing the Marxist creed. But the guilt of the teacher should turn on overt acts. So long as she is a law-abiding citizen, so long as her performance within the public school system meets professional standards, her private life, her political philosophy, her social creed should not be the cause of reprisals against her.

12

Beilan v. Board of Education of Philadelphia

357 U.S. 399 (1958)

Herman A. Beilan, who had been a teacher for twenty-two years in the Philadelphia public school system, refused to answer questions put to him by the Superintendent of Schools regarding alleged past Communist activities. Pursuant to the provisions of the Pennsylvania Public School Code dealing with dismissal proceedings, Beilan was given a formal hearing before the Board of Public Education on the charge that his refusal to answer his Superintendent's questions constituted "incompetency." By a vote of 14 to one, the Board found that the charge of incompetency had been sustained and discharged Beilan from employment as a teacher. In a companion case, Lerner *v.* Casey, *357 U.S. 468 (1958), the Court reviewed the discharge of a subway conductor in the New York City Transit System under the New York Security Risk Law. The conductor had refused to answer a question put to him by his employer as to his membership in the Communist Party, and this was held to be evidence of doubtful trust and reliability. Three Justices dissented in both cases.*

Certiorari to the Supreme Court of Pennsylvania.

MR. JUSTICE BURTON delivered the opinion of the Court.

By engaging in teaching in the public schools, petitioner did not give up his right to freedom of belief, speech or association. He did, however, undertake obligations of frankness, candor and cooperation in answering inquiries made of him by his employing Board examining into his fitness to serve it as a public school teacher.

"A teacher works in a sensitive area in a schoolroom. There he shapes the attitude of young minds toward the society in which they live. In this, the state has a vital concern. It must preserve the integrity of the schools. That the school authorities have the right and the duty to screen the officials, teachers, and employees as to their fitness to maintain the integrity of the schools as a part of ordered society, cannot be doubted." *Adler* v. *Board of Education,* 342 U.S. 485, 493.

As this Court stated in *Garner* v. *Board of Public Works,* 341 U.S. 716, 720, "We think that a municipal employer is not disabled because it is an agency of the State from inquiring of its employees as to matters that may prove relevant to their fitness and suitability for the public service."

The question asked of petitioner by his Superintendent was relevant to the issue of petitioner's fitness and suitability to serve as a teacher. Petitioner is not in a position to challenge his dismissal merely because of the remoteness in time of the 1944 activities. It was apparent from the circumstances of the two interviews that the Superintendent had other questions to ask. Petitioner's refusal to answer was not based on the remoteness of his 1944 activities. He made it clear that he would not answer any question of the same type as the one asked. Petitioner blocked from the beginning any inquiry into his Communist activities, however relevant to his present loyalty. The Board based its dismissal upon petitioner's refusal to answer any inquiry about his relevant activities—not upon those activities themselves. It took care to charge petitioner with incompetency, and not with disloyalty. It found him insubordinate and lacking in frankness and candor—it made no finding as to his loyalty.

We find no requirement in the Federal Constitution that a teacher's classroom conduct be the sole basis for determining his fitness. Fitness for teaching depends on a broad range of factors. The Pennsylvania tenure provision specifies several disqualifying grounds, including immorality, intemperance, cruelty, mental derangement and persistent and willful violation of the school laws, as well as "incompetency." However, the Pennsylvania statute, unlike those of many other States, contains no catch-all phrase such as "conduct unbecoming a teacher," to cover disqualifying conduct not included within the more specific provisions. Consequently, the Pennsylvania courts have given "incompetency" a broad interpretation. . . .

In the instant case, the Pennsylvania Supreme Court has held that "incompetency" includes petitioner's "deliberate and insubordinate refusal to answer the questions of his administrative superior in a vitally important matter pertaining to his fitness." . . . This interpretation is not inconsistent with the Federal Constitution.

Petitioner complains that he was denied due process because he was not sufficiently warned of the consequences of his refusal to answer his Superintendent. The record, however, shows that the Superintendent, in his second interview, specifically warned petitioner that his refusal to answer "was a very serious and a very important matter and that failure to answer the questions might lead to his dismissal." That was sufficient warning to petitioner that his refusal to answer might jeopardize his employment. Furthermore, at petitioner's request, his Superintendent gave him ample opportunity to consult counsel. There was no element of surprise.

Affirmed.

MR. CHIEF JUSTICE WARREN, dissenting.

I believe the facts of record . . . compel the conclusion that Beilan's plea of the Fifth Amendment before a subcommittee of the House Committee on Un-American Activities was so inextricably involved in the Board's decision to discharge him that the validity of the Board's action cannot be sustained without consideration of this ground. The clearest indication of this is the fact that for 13 months following petitioner's refusal to answer the Superintendent's questions, he was retained as a school teacher and continually rated "satisfactory," yet five days after his appearance before the House subcommittee petitioner was suspended. Since a plea of the Fifth Amendment before a congressional committee is an invalid basis for discharge from public employment, *Slochower* v. *Board of Higher Education*, 350 U.S. 551, I would reverse the judgment approving the petitioner's dismissal.

MR. JUSTICE DOUGLAS, with whom MR. JUSTICE BLACK concurs, dissenting.

Among the liberties of the citizens that are guaranteed by the Fourteenth Amendment are those contained in the First Amendment. . . . These include the right to believe what one chooses, the right to differ from his neighbor, the right to pick and choose the political philosophy that he likes best, the right to associate with whomever he chooses, the right to join the groups he prefers, the privilege of selecting his own path to salvation. . . .

We deal here only with a matter of belief. We have no evidence in either case that the employee in question ever committed a crime, ever moved in treasonable opposition against this country. The only mark against them—if it can be called such—is a refusal to answer questions concerning Communist Party membership. This is said to give rise to doubts concerning the competence of the teacher in the *Beilan* case and doubts as to the trustworthiness and reliability of the subway conductor in the *Lerner* case.

Our legal system is premised on the theory that every person is innocent until he is proved guilty. In this country we have, however, been moving away from that concept. We have been generating the belief that anyone who remains silent when interrogated about his unpopular beliefs or affiliations is guilty. I would allow no inference of wrongdoing to flow from the invocation of any constitutional right. I would not let that principle bow to popular passions. For all we know we are dealing here with citizens who are wholly innocent of any wrongful action. That must indeed be our premise. When we make the contrary assumption, we part radically with our tradition.

If it be said that we deal not with guilt or innocence but with frankness, the answer is the same. There are areas where government may not probe. Private citizens, private clubs, private groups may make such deductions and reach such conclusions as they choose from the failure of a citizen to disclose his beliefs, his philosophy, his associates. But government has no business penalizing a citizen merely for his beliefs or associations. . . .

If we break with tradition and let the government penalize these citizens for their beliefs and associations, the most we can assume from their failure to answer is that they were Communists. Yet, as we said in *Wieman* v. *Updegraff,* 344 U.S. 183, 190, membership in the Communist Party "may be innocent." The member may have thought that the Communist movement would develop in the parliamentary tradition here, or he may not have been aware of any unlawful aim, or knowing it, may have embraced only the socialist philosophy of the group, not any political tactics of violence and terror. Many join associations, societies, and fraternities with less than full endorsement of all their aims.

We compound error in these decisions. We not only impute wrongdoing to those who invoke their constitutional rights. We go further and impute the worst possible motives to them. . . .

In sum, we have here only a bare refusal to testify; and the Court holds that sufficient to show that these employees are unfit to hold their public posts. That makes qualification for public office turn solely on a matter of belief—a notion very much at war with the Bill of Rights.

When we make the belief of the citizens the basis of government action, we move toward the concept of *total security.* Yet *total security* is possible only in a totalitarian regime—the kind of system we profess to combat.

MR. JUSTICE BRENNAN, dissenting.

This Court refuses to pierce the transparent denials that each of these employees was publicly branded disloyal. The Court holds that we are bound by the definition of state law pronounced by the States' high courts that the dismissals were for unreliability and incompetency. Of course, we accept state law as the high court of a State pronounces it, but certainly our duty to secure to the individual the safeguards, embodied in due process, against a State's arbitrary exercise of power is no less when the state courts refuse to recognize what has in fact occurred. . . . In my view the judgments in both cases must be reversed because each petitioner has been branded a disloyal American without the due process of law required of the States by the Fourteenth Amendment. . . .

I might agree that the Due Process Clause imposes no restraint against dismissal of a teacher who refuses to answer his superior's questions asked in the privacy of his office and related to the teacher's fitness to continue in his position.

But in reality Beilan was not dismissed by the Pennsylvania school authorities upon that ground. The question whether he had been an officer in the Communist Party in 1944 was first asked of Beilan by the Superintendent at a private interview on June 25, 1952. Beilan did not refuse at that time to answer but asked permission to consult counsel. The Superintendent summoned him again on October 14, 1952, and it was on that date that Beilan advised the Superintendent that he declined to answer that or similar questions. The Superintendent had told Beilan at the first interview that the question was asked because the Superintendent had information which reflected on Beilan's loyalty. Almost fourteen months elapsed before Beilan was suspended and the charges preferred which led to his dismissal. In that interval Beilan's superiors had twice rated him in the high satisfactory range of competency. Had the authorities seriously regarded Beilan as incompetent because of his refusal to answer the Superintendent's question they would hardly have waited so long before suspending him. The record is clear that proceedings were actually initiated not because of that refusal to answer but because on November 18, 1953, Beilan asserted the privilege against self-incrimination under the Fifth Amendment when interrogated at a publicly televised hearing held in Philadelphia by a Subcommittee of the Committee on Un-American Activities of the House of Representatives. Beilan testified at that hearing that he was not then a member of the Communist Party and had never advocated the overthrow of the Government by force or violence but pleaded the protection of the Fifth Amendment when asked questions directed to past party membership and activities. Five days later, on November 23, 1953, the Superintendent notified Beilan that he had been rated "unsatisfactory" because he had refused to answer the Superintendent's question and also because "you invoked the Fifth Amendment of the Federal Constitution" when questioned as to "past associations with organizations of doubtful loyalty" by the Subcommittee. The opinion on Beilan's administrative appeal which sustained his dismissal by the Board of Education makes it clear that the authorities viewed Beilan's invocation of the Fifth Amendment before the Subcommittee as an admission of disloyalty. . . .

13

Barenblatt v. United States

360 U.S. 109 (1959)

Barenblatt had been a graduate student and teaching fellow at the University of Michigan from 1947 to 1950, and an instructor in psychology at Vassar College from 1950 until shortly before his appearance before a Subcommittee of the House Committee on Un-American Activities. The Subcommittee was engaged in an inquiry concerning alleged Communist infiltration into the field of education. Barenblatt refused to answer questions regarding present or past membership in the Communist Party or in affiliated organizations. He expressly disclaimed reliance upon the Self-Incrimination Clause of the Fifth Amendment, relying mainly upon the First Amendment guaranty of freedom of speech, religion and association. Convicted of contempt of Congress, he brought this appeal to the Supreme Court. The Court affirmed the conviction below, holding (1) that the statutory charter of authority of the Committee was not unconstitutionally vague, and that the House of Representatives had never regarded the field of education as being outside the Committee's authority; (2) that the petitioner had been properly apprised of the pertinency of the Subcommittee's questions to the subject matter of the inquiry; and (3) that First Amendment rights were not infringed. Portions of the opinion dealing only with the third issue are reproduced here.

Certiorari to the U.S. Court of Appeals for the District of Columbia.

MR. JUSTICE HARLAN delivered the opinion of the Court.

In the present case congressional efforts to learn the extent of a nationwide, indeed worldwide, problem have brought one of its investigating committees into the field of education. Of course, broadly viewed, inquiries cannot be made into the teaching that is pursued in any of our educational institutions. When academic teaching-freedom and its corollary learning-freedom, so essential to the well-being of the Nation, are claimed, this Court will always be on the alert against intrusion by Congress into this constitutionally protected domain. But this does not mean that the Congress is precluded from interrogating a witness merely because he is a teacher. An educational institution is not a constitutional sanctuary from inquiry into matters that may otherwise be within the constitutional legislative domain merely for the reason that inquiry is made of someone within its walls. . . .

The Court's past cases establish sure guides to decision. Undeniably, the First Amendment in some circumstances protects an individual from being compelled to disclose his associational relationships. However, the protections of the First Amendment, unlike a proper claim of the privilege against self-incrimination under the Fifth Amendment, do not afford a witness the right to resist inquiry in all circumstances. Where First Amendment rights are asserted to bar governmental interrogation resolution of the issue always involves a balancing by the courts of the competing private and public interests at stake in the particular circumstances shown. . . .

The first question is whether this investigation was related to a valid legislative purpose, for Congress may not constitutionally require an individual to disclose his political relationships or other private affairs except in relation to such a purpose. . . .

That Congress has wide power to legislate in the field of Communist activity in this Country, and to conduct appropriate investigations in aid thereof, is hardly debatable. The existence of such power has never been questioned by this Court, and it is sufficient to say, without particularization, that Congress has enacted or considered in this field a wide range of legislative measures, not a few of which have stemmed from recommendations of the very Committee whose actions have been drawn in question here. In the last analysis this power rests on the right of self-preservation, "the ultimate value of any society." . . . Justification for its exercise in turn rests on the long and widely accepted view that the tenets of the Communist Party include the ultimate overthrow of the Government of the United States by force and violence, a view which has been given formal expression by the Congress.

On these premises, this Court in its constitutional adjudications has consistently refused to view the Communist Party as an ordinary political party, and has upheld federal legislation aimed at the Communist problem which in a different context would certainly have raised constitutional issues of the gravest character. . . . On the same premises this Court has upheld under the Fourteenth Amendment state legislation requiring those occupying or seeking public office to disclaim knowing membership in any organization advocating overthrow of the Government by force and violence, which legislation none can avoid seeing was aimed at membership in the Communist Party. . . . Similarly, in other areas, this Court has recognized the close nexus between the Communist Party and violent overthrow of government. . . . To suggest that because the Communist Party may also sponsor peaceable political reforms the constitutional issues before us should now be judged as if that Party were just an ordinary political party from the standpoint of national security, is to ask this Court to blind itself to world affairs which have determined the whole course of our national policy since the close of World War II.

We think that investigatory power in this domain is not to be denied Congress solely because the field of education is involved. Nothing in the prevailing opinions in *Sweezy* v. *State of New Hampshire* stands for a contrary view. The vice existing there was that the questioning of Sweezy, who had not been shown ever to have been connected with the Communist Party, as to the contents of a lecture he had given at the University of New Hampshire, and as to his connections with the Progressive Party, then on the ballot as a normal political party in some 26 States, was too far removed from the premises on which the constitutionality of the State's investigation had to depend to withstand attack under the Fourteenth Amendment. . . . This is a very different thing from inquiring into the extent to which the Communist Party has succeeded in infiltrating into our universities, or elsewhere, persons and groups committed to furthering the objective of overthrow. . . . Indeed we do not understand petitioner here to suggest that Congress in no circumstances may inquire into Communist activity in the field of education. Rather, his position is in effect that this particular investigation was aimed not at the revolutionary aspects but at the theoretical classroom discussion of communism.

In our opinion this position rests on a too constricted view of the nature of the investigatory process, and is not supported by a fair assessment of the record before us. An investigation of advocacy of or preparation for overthrow certainly embraces the right to identify a witness as a member of the Communist Party, . . . and to inquire into the various manifestations of the Party's tenets. The strict requirements of a prosecution under the Smith Act . . . are not the measure of the permissible scope of a congressional investigation into "overthrow," for of necessity the investigatory process must proceed step by step. Nor can it fairly be concluded that this investigation was directed at controlling what is being taught at our universities rather than at overthrow. The statement of the Subcommittee Chairman at the opening of the investigation evinces no such intention, and so far as this record reveals nothing thereafter transpired which would justify our holding that the thrust of the investigation later changed. The record discloses considerable testimony concerning the foreign domination and revolutionary purposes and efforts of the Communist Party. That there was also testimony on the abstract philosophical level does not detract from the dominant theme of this investigation—Communist infiltration furthering the alleged ultimate purpose of overthrow. And certainly the conclusion would not be justified that the questioning of petitioner would have exceeded permissible bounds had he not shut off the Subcommittee at the threshold.

Nor can we accept the further contention that this investigation should not be deemed to have been in furtherance of a legislative purpose because the true objective of the Committee and of the Congress was purely "exposture." So long as Congress acts in pursuance of its constitutional power, the Judiciary lacks authority to intervene on the basis of the motives which spurred the exercise of that power.

Affirmed.

MR. JUSTICE BLACK, with whom the CHIEF JUSTICE, and MR. JUSTICE DOUGLAS concur, dissenting.

The First Amendment says in no equivocal language that Congress shall pass no law abridging freedom of speech, press, assembly or petition. The activities of this Committee, authorized by Congress, do precisely that, through exposure, obloquy and public scorn. . . . The Court does not really deny this fact but relies on a combination of three reasons for permitting the infringement: (A) The notion that despite the First Amendment's command Congress can abridge speech and association if this Court decides that the governmental interest in abridging speech is greater than an individual's interest in exercising that freedom; (B) the Government's right to "preserve itself"; (C) the fact that the Committee is only after Communists or suspected Communists in this investigation.

(A) I do not agree that laws directly abridging First Amendment freedoms can be justified by a congressional or judicial balancing process. . . .

To apply the Court's balancing test under such circumstances is to read the First Amendment to say "Congress shall pass no law abridging freedom of speech, press, assembly and petition, unless Congress and the

Supreme Court reach the joint conclusion that on balance the interests of the Government in stifling these freedoms is greater than the interest of the people in having them exercised." This is closely akin to the notion that neither the First Amendment nor any other provision of the Bill of Rights should be enforced unless the Court believes it is *reasonable* to do so. Not only does this violate the genius of our *written* Constitution, but it runs expressly counter to the injunction to Court and Congress made by Madison when he introduced the Bill of Rights. . . .

But even assuming what I cannot assume, that some balancing is proper in this case, I feel that the Court after stating the test ignores it completely. At most it balances the right of the Government to preserve itself, against Barenblatt's right to refrain from revealing Communist affiliations. Such a balance, however, mistakes the factors to be weighed. In the first place, it completely leaves out the real interest in Barenblatt's silence, the interest of the people as a whole in being able to join organizations, advocate causes and make political "mistakes" without later being subjected to governmental penalties for having dared to think for themselves. It is this right, the right to err politically, which keeps us strong as a Nation. For no number of laws against communism can have as much effect as the personal conviction which comes from having heard its arguments and rejected them, or from having once accepted its tenets and later recognized their worthlessness. Instead, the obloquy which results from investigations such as this not only stifles "mistakes" but prevents all but the most courageous from hazarding any views which might at some later time become disfavored. This result, whose importance cannot be overestimated, is doubly crucial when it affects the universities, on which we must largely rely for the experimentation and development of new ideas essential to our country's welfare. It is these interests of society, rather than Barenblatt's own right to silence, which I think the Court should put on the balance against the demands of the

Government, if any balancing process is to be tolerated. Instead they are not mentioned, while on the other side the demands of the Government are vastly overstated and called "self preservation." It is admitted that this Committee can only seek information for the purpose of suggesting laws, and that Congress' power to make laws in the realm of speech and association is quite limited, even on the Court's test. Its interest in making such laws in the field of education, primarily a state function, is clearly narrower still. Yet the Court styles this attenuated interest self-preservation and allows it to overcome the need our country has to let us all think, speak, and associate politically as we like and without fear of reprisal. . . .

(B) Moreover, I cannot agree with the Court's notion that First Amendment freedoms must be abridged in order to "preserve" our country. That notion rests on the unarticulated premise that this Nation's security hangs upon its power to punish people because of what they think, speak or write about, or because of those with whom they associate for political purposes. The Government, in its brief, virtually admits this position when it speaks of the "communication of unlawful ideas." I challenge this premise, and deny that ideas can be proscribed under our Constitution. I agree that despotic governments cannot exist without stifling the voice of opposition to their oppressive practices. The First Amendment means to me, however, that the only constitutional way our Government can preserve itself is to leave its people the fullest possible freedom to praise, criticize or discuss, as they see fit, all governmental policies and to suggest, if they desire, that even its most fundamental postulates are bad and should be changed. . . . On that premise this land was created, and on that premise it has grown to greatness. Our Constitution assumes that the common sense of the people and their attachment to our country will enable them, after free discussion, to withstand ideas that are wrong. To say that our patriotism must be protected against false ideas by means other than these is, I think, to make a baseless charge. . . .

(C) The Court implies, however, that the ordinary rules and requirements of the Constitution do not apply because the Committee is merely after Communists and they do not constitute a political party but only a criminal gang. . . .

No matter how often or how quickly we repeat the claim that the Communist Party is not a political party, we cannot outlaw it, as a group, without endangering the liberty of all of us. The reason is not hard to find, for mixed among those aims of communism which are illegal are perfectly normal political and social goals. And muddled with its revolutionary tenets is a drive to achieve power through the ballot, if it can be done. These things necessarily make it a political party whatever other, illegal, aims it may have. . . .

The fact is that once we allow any group which has some political aims or ideas to be driven from the ballot and from the battle for men's minds because some of its members are bad and some of its tenets are illegal, no group is safe. . . .

MR. JUSTICE BRENNAN, dissenting.

I would reverse this conviction. It is sufficient that I state my complete agreement with my Brother BLACK that no purpose for the investigation of Barenblatt is revealed by the record except exposure purely for the sake of exposure. This is not a purpose to which Barenblatt's rights under the First Amendment can validly be subordinated. An investigation in which the processes of law-making and law-evaluating are submerged entirely in exposure of individual behavior—in adjudication, of a sort, through the exposure process—is outside the constitutional pale of congressional inquiry. . . .